Country Flags: Worst to Best

Max Hall

DEDICATION

For Solmaz, Michael and Tim, who inspired me to write
this book in the first place.

CONTENTS

PREFACE

In this book, I will be attempting to rank the flags of every country in the world from worst to best, according to various principles which have been established in the field of vexillology (that is, the study of flags). The following list is the result of this project, which I have been working on for the past few years and have taken the time in the current coronavirus epidemic to complete. I hope you enjoy this list and are able to learn a thing or two about flags in the process.

Firstly, however, I would like to illustrate in this preface how I attempted to quantify and rank the quality of each flag.

One of the best resources for any budding vexillologist has got to be Ted Kaye's Good Flag, Bad Flag, which can be accessed through the North American Vexillological Association (NAVA), and I would thoroughly recommend reading for yourself regardless of what you think of my list (it's a short read and free to access in several languages). In this book, Kaye suggests five key principles for good flag design, and illustrates this with various national, state and city flags. These principles have served as the main inspiration for the following categories, in which every flag has been rated, with the total scores providing the list seen in this book.

Category 1: Colour Scheme
(rated out of 20)

Not as significant as the other categories here, but still very important, three factors are taken into account here:

- Are the colours from the basic palette suggested by Kaye (red, white, blue, green, yellow, black)?
- Do the colours work well together?
- How many colours are there? (Should not typically be more than 2 or 3 main colours).

Other factors, such as the symbolism behind these colours, or the distinctiveness provided by them, are not considered for this category as they are encompassed by others.

Category 2: Identifiability
(rated out of 40)

The ability to recognise a nations flag is one of the most important aspects of flag design, and something every country should aim for. Scores have been applied based on the following criteria:

- Is the flag distinctive? This is considering the colour scheme, design, etc., and is relative to how well-known the country is to the rest of the world (for instance, although many will not be familiar with Vanuatu, their flag does well to make it memorable for the viewer).
- If not, is it similar to other national flags for good reason (e.g. historical context behind flags with the Nordic cross or 'Pan-Arab' colours)?
- Minor consideration for the longevity of the flag (e.g. Afghanistan's flag being subject to frequent changes, making it more difficult to become familiar with their flag).

Category 3: Design
(rated out of 40)

Crucial to the success of a flag is its design, assessed by the criteria below:

- Meaningful symbolism behind the design, including the colour scheme (and is this obvious from looking at the flag?).
- Aspect ratios/shape (generally irrelevant, but do distinctly shaped flags have a good reason for doing so?
- "Keep it simple"! One of the most frequent issues you will see with many of the flags in the bottom half of this list is a frustrating tendency to use the coat of arms of their nation, which are usually extraordinarily complex, and remains one of the laziest tropes of flag design. The same applies for flags with unnecessary text, or the Union Jack in the corner.

After rating a flag in these categories, this gives us a total score out of 100, from which the following list has been produced. All given scores are whole numbers, and clearly there are more than 100 countries, so in the inevitable event of a draw, I have made an educated judgement based on these factors to decide which flag comes out on top.

It may seem that a disproportionate number of flags have scored over 50/100, but the reason for this is simple, being that the bar for national flag design is set rather high, and most flags have enough redeeming qualities to carry them over the 50% threshold.

DISCLAIMERS

Let's address the most obvious disclaimer first: what countries will be included in this list?

The simplest answer is if it's a UN member state, it counts, bringing the total number of countries included up to 193. This is to avoid any potential controversy in which nations I have or have not included. In addition, there are four more countries which have been included in this list. The first two of these, Vatican City and Palestine, are officially UN 'observer states', whilst the remaining two (Kosovo and Taiwan) have been included due to their membership of one or more of the specialised agencies in the UN. This brings the total up to 197.

To clarify, the following states have not been included for these reasons:

- Cook Islands and Niue, despite their membership of UN specialised agencies, as they are in free association with New Zealand.
- States including Western Sahara and Northern Cyprus, despite recognition from other nations, as they have no membership in the UN.
- States including Somaliland and Artsakh, as they have no recognition from any UN member states.
- The 'countries' of the United Kingdom (England, Wales, Scotland and Northern Ireland), as they are constituents of a larger country, and not UN members in their own right.
- Overseas territories of UN member states, such as Gibraltar (UK) and Puerto Rico (US).

The other main disclaimer that must be made before I delve into the list is as follows:

A country's placement on this list has <u>no relation</u> to the quality of its government, its stances on social or political issues, or any other factor that might make a country 'good' or 'bad'.

The purpose of this list has nothing to do with any of these issues, it is simply an attempt to use established vexillological principles to try to quantify how successful each national flag is at this. Please consider this if you see a country that you particularly like place low down on this list, and vice versa.

It is also worth saying that, although an attempt has been made here to be as objective and unbiased as possible, you may disagree with some of these placements, and that's okay! I am not claiming that this list is 100%, categorically correct, but a great deal of care and attention has gone into crafting it, so hopefully you will find yourself agreeing with most placements.

With all of this in mind, let's get into the rankings...

197 - HAITI

Colour: 6   Design: 6

Identifiability: 10

Total: 22/100

The flag of Haiti is truly deserving of the last place in this list. Upon discovering in the 1936 Berlin Olympics that they had the same plain red and blue flag as Liechtenstein, both countries decided to add a distinguishing feature to their flags. Liechtenstein certainly got the better side of this deal, with Haiti opting to adorn their flag with a tiny coat of arms, complete with white background, that looks as though someone designed it using archaic computer software.

196 - MONACO

Colour: 14   Design: 4

Identifiability: 5

Total: 23/100

Deciding between the next three positions was a challenge, due to their similarity - in fact, the flags of Monaco and Indonesia would be the same were it not for the squarer 4:5 ratio that Monaco opted for. Monaco's flag is uninspired and hard to distinguish, not only from Indonesia and Poland, but many other national flags too, and combined with it ignoring flag conventions and being formatted to an unusual ratio, Monaco lands the penultimate place on this list.

195 - INDONESIA

Colour: 14   Design: 5

Identifiability: 5

Total: 24/100

The only thing giving the flag of Indonesia an upper hand compared to Monaco is the historical significance of the colours red and white slightly outweighing those of Monaco, and that the flag is a more conventional shape. Other than that, you don't need me to tell you that this flag is boring.

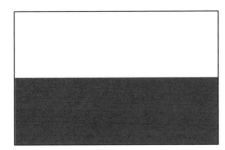

194 - POLAND

Colour: 14   Design: 5

Identifiability: 7

Total: 26/100

At least the red and white have been switched around for the Poland flag, making it slightly more unique than the flags of Indonesia and Monaco. With that aside, the Poland flag really doesn't have much going for it, beside (once again) the historical significance of red and white.

193 - BENIN

Colour: 12   Design: 9

Identifiability: 6

Total: 27/100

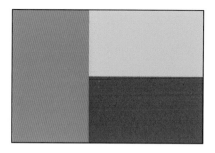

The flag of this West African nation has to be one of the most forgettable national flags in the world, and with almost no indication of what country is being represented by this flag, you would be hard-pressed to make any informed guess that this is the flag of Benin. Saving this flag from the bottom 3 in this list is the distinctly African colour scheme, and the slightly more unusual pattern than the standard tricolour.

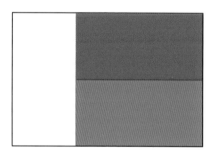

192 - MADAGASCAR

Colour: 14   Design: 10

Identifiability: 5

Total: 29/100

Much like the flag of Benin, Madagascar's flag tells you virtually nothing about the country in question. The Madagascan flag is only ranked slightly higher due to an arguably more aesthetically pleasing colour scheme, and the use of red and white linking the flag to Indonesia, where Madagascar's first settlers travelled from.

191 - MALDIVES

Colour: 9   Design: 9

Identifiability: 14

Total: 32/100

While many countries in the bottom quarter of this list give little indication of where in the world the countries they represent are, the Maldives go a step further, with a flag that is actively confusing, and would certainly not imply that is represents an island nation in the Indian Ocean. Not the mention the boring and uninformative flag design demonstrated here. Poor showing from the Maldives.

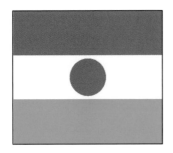

190 - NIGER

Colour: 11   Design: 14

Identifiability: 7

Total: 32/100

Niger's flag doesn't do this Saharan nation any justice, instead it looks like a budget version of the far more famous Indian flag. Niger would greatly benefit from a complete redesign of their flag - something that would get itself noticed on the world stage.

189 - EQUATORIAL GUINEA

Colour: 7   Design: 7

Identifiability: 18

Total: 32/100

Equatorial Guinea's flag can be adequately described in one word: 'messy'. The colours clash with each other, the coat of arms adds too much unnecessary detail to the flag, and text featuring in a country's flag is generally not a good sign. All of this comes together to make a flag that most people would still be unable to recognise.

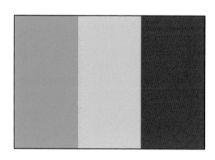

188 - MALI

Colour: 10   Design: 12

Identifiability: 11

Total: 33/100

Far from the most unique flag, there isn't much to say about Mali's tricolour. It is worth noting the distinctively African colour scheme, which when combined with the French-inspired tricolour design, is at least able to say something of the country in question, as an African nation previously colonised by France.

187 - LIECHTENSTEIN

Colour: 7   Design: 15

Identifiability: 12

Total: 34/100

At the 1936 Berlin Olympics, Liechtenstein realised that they were using the same flag as Haiti (197th in this list), which led to the placement of a crown in the top-left corner. Whilst this arguably gives the flag of Liechtenstein more meaningful imagery, the colours still clash with each other, and the crown is far too detailed.

186 - AUSTRIA

Colour: 14   Design: 12

Identifiability: 9

Total: 35/100

Austria's flag isn't bad, but it is far from being unique, and could easily be confused with a lot of other national flags. The choice of colour is boring, and with no details or imagery, this flag says very little for Austria, which has had a long and detailed history.

185 - LATVIA

Colour: 9   Design: 12

Identifiability: 14

Total: 35/100

Remarkably similar to the flag of Austria (186th), Latvia's flag is for the most part fairly unnoteworthy, with the main exception of the darker red colour, relatively uncommon amongst national flags. Typically, it is preferable for a flag to use more regular colours, however when contrasted to the flag of Austria, Latvia's flag is clearly a bit more defined, resulting in its higher placement.

184 - BOLIVIA

Colour: 12   Design: 13

Identifiability: 10

Total: 35/100

Bolivia's flag sometimes features a coat of arms in the center, but for the purposes of this book, I have decided to rank the version without this overly detailed motif, to give it the best chance of success in this list. Evidently, by its placement in 184th, this hasn't made a huge difference, and I am sure you can appreciate why. Bolivia's flag is, for want of a better word, boring, especially when you consider some of the other flags in South America.

183 - TURKMENISTAN

Colour: 6   Design: 9

Identifiability: 20

Total: 35/100

Picture the scene: You're a pupil at a Turkmen school, learning about the history of your country, and your teacher asks you to draw the flag of Turkmenistan. Suddenly, you begin to resent the fact that your flag features five intricately designed traditional carpets stacked on top of each other.

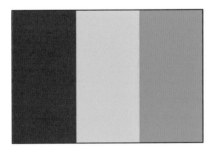

182 - GUINEA

Colour: 15   Design: 13

Identifiability: 9

Total: 37/100

Very similar to the flag of Mali (188th), this flag says just as little for Guinea. The darker green used here at least makes the flag stand out a bit more, and Guinea's flag is slightly older too, giving it the upper hand. Besides this, there is little to say for this flag.

181 - MAURITANIA

Colour: 8   Design: 15

Identifiability: 14

Total: 37/100

The Mauritanian flag is one of the most recent flags to be changed, updated in late 2017 with the addition of two red stripes to symbolise the blood spilled in defence against the French colonialists in this Saharan nation. Whilst the additional detail in this flag was well-needed, I suspect Mauritania didn't take this far enough, and would still benefit from some more defining features.

180 - PERU

Colour: 14   Design: 15

Identifiability: 9

Total: 38/100

Much like bordering Bolivia (184th), the Peruvian flag is a rare example of a South American flag done badly. Peru had so many options for an interesting and exciting flag, whether depicting the rich culture of its people or the diversity of its landscape, yet instead chose this vague and forgettable flag to represent their nation. Not an ugly flag by any means, but largely characterless.

179 - MOROCCO

Colour: 7   Design: 14

Identifiability: 18

Total: 39/100

Perhaps further down this list than some might expect, the flag of Morocco has one main advantage, being among the more recognisable flags of Western Africa. With that said, this flag suffers heavily from a boring design and a poor colour scheme, with the red and green both being too dark and clashing with each other.

178 - BELIZE

Colour: 7   Design: 6

Identifiability: 26

Total: 39/100

Any potentially redeeming qualities about the flag of Belize are thrown out the window when you consider the enormous coat of arms that dominates the center, which is far too detailed for a national flag. As a result, Belize's flag ends up having more in common with many of the excessive and frustrating U.S. state flags than it does with its Central American neighbours, and is memorable only because of how over-the-top its design is. On the plus side, Belize is noteworthy for being the only national flag to feature humans as a significant part of its design, with the exception of Malta (172nd), with a small depiction of St. George.

177 - LUXEMBOURG

Colour: 16   Design: 16

Identifiability: 8

Total: 40/100

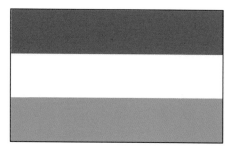

Luxembourg's flag is actually pretty old, so you may expect it to place a little higher in this list due to the history surrounding it, however its striking similarity with the even older Dutch flag (111th) cannot be overlooked, and has been the subject of debate to get the flag changed. When the most notable thing about your flag is how similar it looks to a preexisting country flag, that can't be a good sign.

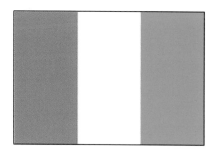

176 - IVORY COAST

Colour: 15   Design: 16

Identifiability: 8

Total: 40/100

The first thing you will probably notice about the flag of the Ivory Coast is how much it looks like the Irish flag (46th). I'm not for a moment suggesting that Ireland somehow has a monopoly over these colours, but with the Irish flag predating the Ivorian one by several decades at the least, you must wonder if there would have been a better option for the Ivory Coast to adopt.

175 - UKRAINE

Colour: 15   Design: 7

Identifiability: 18

Total: 40/100

Let's be honest: flags like that of Ukraine, which have only two plain colours, are really boring. What Ukraine's flag does do however, is represent a view of the sky over a field of wheat, which is at least an interesting concept. Besides this, the Ukrainian flag is certainly one of the lazier appearing designs, and would not look out of place as a beach safety flag.

174 - SOUTH SUDAN

Colour: 6   Design: 14

Identifiability: 21

Total: 41/100

The flag of South Sudan, the world's newest country, suffers from one major issue - it has too many colours. South Sudan were trying to say too much with their flag, and as a result, it comes across as messy and confusing. The blue and yellow chevron is the main culprit for this, appearing forced and out-of-place. A more basic design incorporating the black, red and green tricolour would be preferable.

173 - MOLDOVA

Colour: 14 Design: 12

Identifiability: 16

Total: 42/100

Moldova's flag shares its colour scheme with the flags of Andorra, Chad and Romania, only having any significant historical link to the latter. This might not have been problematic, if it had anything other than its blocky coat of arms to differentiate itself from these flags. As a relatively new country, gaining independence from the USSR in 1991, it is fair to say that these other nations have had longer to establish their flags, so Moldova could have benefitted from a different design.

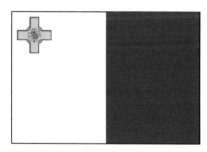

172 - MALTA

Colour: 12   Design: 15

Identifiability: 15

Total: 42/100

Malta's flag is yet another red and white European flag, although unlike the likes of Monaco and Poland, the design at least has something to distinguish itself from the crowd, that being the George Cross on the hoist side. Whilst the story behind the George Cross is significant for the history of Malta, representing the award presented to the people of Malta by King George VI of the UK, its detailed design and the colour grey used contribute to the overall dull appearance of this flag.

171 - TAIWAN

Colour: 8   Design: 19

Identifiability: 15

Total: 42/100

The flag of Taiwan, officially the Republic of China, is at best pleasant, and at worst forgettable, with vague imagery, and little to suggest that this is the flag of Taiwan. The rays around the sun supposedly represent 'shíchén', an archaic unit to measure time, of which there were twelve in a day, but besides this, Taiwan's flag has just the colours chosen to represent their nation, of which they have picked some of the most common.

170 - EL SALVADOR

Colour: 14   Design: 14

Identifiability: 14

Total: 42/100

The flags of the Central American nations of El Salvador, Nicaragua (166th) and Honduras (137th) can be very easily confused with each other. Whilst similarities between flags can be a useful tool for depicting the shared values or history between countries, it is plain to see that these flags have taken it too far. Ranking in last place out of these nations is the flag of El Salvador, as it was adopted the latest of these three flags, so they had plenty of time to design a better one.

169 - ZAMBIA

Colour: 4   Design: 13

Identifiability: 26

Total: 43/100

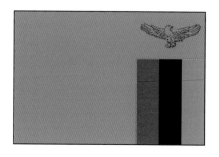

The flag of Zambia ranks 197th out of 197 for the 'colour' category, and I hope you can see why. It's hard to tell what Zambia was really going for with this design, and as a result, the flag ends up looking ill-conceived and messy. With that said, it's certainly distinctive, and looks very little like any other national flag.

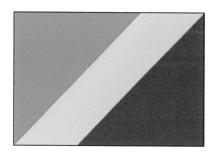

168 - REPUBLIC OF THE CONGO

Colour: 12   Design: 18

Identifiability: 13

Total: 43/100

The flag of the Republic of the Congo, not to be confused with the bordering Democratic Republic of the Congo (8th), places an astonishing 160 places behind its similarly named neighbour, and for good reason. Besides from the use of diagonals, it is remarkably similar to other nearby nations, with essentially no imagery or iconography to suggest what nation it represents. The use of a distinctively African colour scheme is helpful however.

167 - SAMOA

Colour: 8   Design: 19

Identifiability: 16

Total: 43/100

The Samoan flag design is very similar to that of Taiwan (171st) and was first designed a few decades after the Taiwanese one, however the Samoan flag is at least a little more helpful in indicating the country it represents. This is thanks mostly to the 'Southern Cross' constellation in the upper hoist side, used by other nations in Oceania (most famously Australia), providing a useful link for Samoa to these nations.

166 - NICARAGUA

Colour: 14   Design: 14

Identifiability: 15

Total: 43/100

As discussed for El Salvador (170th), several of the nations in Central America have frustratingly similar flags to each other, and Nicaragua is another example of this. The flag first saw use over a century ago, yet its longevity hasn't helped the flag become much more recognisable, due to its indistinct design with just a coat of arms to distinguish itself. As a side note, Nicaragua's flag is one of just two national flags to feature the colour purple (the other is Dominica), although only in the rainbow in the center.

165 - FIJI

Colour: 8   Design: 14

Identifiability: 21

Total: 43/100

Many of the Pacific island nations fly some of the best flags the world has to offer. Not Fiji though, made even more disappointing as the nation was set to officially change their flag just a few years ago, but the change was abandoned by their president after Fiji won their first gold medal in the 2016 Olympics, with Fijians proudly flying their flag.

164 - ANDORRA

Colour: 15   Design: 12

Identifiability: 16

Total: 43/100

Continuing a trend of small European nations with unoriginal flag designs, Andorra shares the colours on its flag with several other countries in Europe and beyond, none of which are located anywhere near Andorra. These colours do however hold important historical significance for Andorra, but this flag's rank is held down by the unnecessary inclusion of the country's coat of arms.

163 - BURKINA FASO

Colour: 13   Design: 15

Identifiability: 15

Total: 43/100

It is difficult to find what there is to say about the flag of Burkina Faso, as it hasn't blatantly copied the flag of any other country, but it doesn't exactly stand out from the crowd either. The use of the 'Pan-African' colours is beneficial, but otherwise, Burkina Faso's flag doesn't say very much.

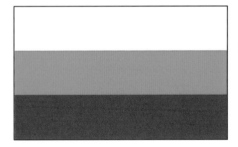

162 - BULGARIA

Colour: 15   Design: 15

Identifiability: 14

Total: 44/100

Bulgaria's flag isn't awful - far from it - but it does little to stand out from the plethora of tricolour flags in Eastern Europe, and would likely benefit from some sort of emblem or insignia to differentiate it from its neighbours The colour choice, however, serves Bulgaria well, as these colours have represented it for over a century, and have become closely connected to Bulgaria.

161 - DOMINICA

Colour: 6   Design: 13

Identifiability: 26

Total: 45/100

Amongst a batch of high-quality, thoughtfully designed flags in the Caribbean, Dominica's flag sticks out like a sore thumb, and is an uncomfortable mismatch of different designs and patterns. Interestingly, this is one of just two national flags to feature the colour purple, although the other (Nicaragua) only features it as part of a rainbow.

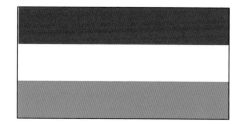

160 - HUNGARY

Colour: 15   Design: 16

Identifiability: 14

Total: 45/100

Hungary's flag is little more than yet another European tricolour, and could easily be confused with a number of other nations. Not a particularly original flag, although the colours used date back several hundred years, and have a cultural significance for Hungary, so at least it has that going for it.

159 - SENEGAL

Colour: 10   Design: 17

Identifiability: 18

Total: 45/100

The flag of Senegal is similar to a number of others in Western Africa, including nearby Mali (188th) and Guinea (182nd), although thankfully for Senegal, it at least has a bit of detail in the form of a star in its center. The similar colours were chosen to represent Senegal's unity with the other nations in the area.

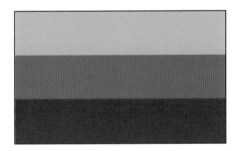

158 - LITHUANIA

Colour: 11   Design: 15

Identifiability: 19

Total: 45/100

In case you haven't already noticed, many of the European tricolour flags will be featuring in the bottom half of this list, and Lithuania's flag is no exception. The fact is, without a distinctive colour scheme, these flags have little to differentiate themselves from each other. With that in mind, Lithuania's flag ranks higher than flags such as Bulgaria's (162nd) and Hungary's (160th) thanks mostly to the yellow making the flag at least a little different.

157 - LAOS

Colour: 8   Design: 21

Identifiability: 16

Total: 45/100

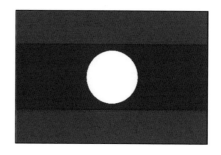

The Laotian flag is a little on the basic side, although the symbolism behind the design is appealing and likeable, supposedly representing the moon shining on the Mekong River. Other than this, the flag of Laos is easy to overlook, and would benefit from some more striking or eye-catching imagery.

156 - SAUDI ARABIA

Colour: 14   Design: 5

Identifiability: 27

Total: 46/100

It should be clear by this point that no amount of text, no matter how important to a given country, should typically be featured in a country's flag. Considering this, Saudi Arabia's flag is mostly text, and I'm sure you can appreciate why this rule of not having text in your flag is a sensible one, as it looks far too elaborate.

155 - GUATEMALA

Colour: 14   Design: 15

Identifiability: 17

Total: 46/100

Among the flags of Central America, Guatemala's flag could certainly be worse, mostly aided by the vertical stripes adopted in this flag, which helpfully distinguish it from the flags of Nicaragua, Honduras and El Salvador which have blue and white horizontal stripes. Clearly however, the emblem in the center adds a lot of unnecessary detail, which could have otherwise been avoided.

154 - VIETNAM

Colour: 13   Design: 19

Identifiability: 15

Total: 47/100

One of the more thoughtfully designed flags in the bottom quarter of this list, Vietnam's flag is illustrative of the political turmoil the nation was in during the 1950s when this flag was designed, and the blood spilled during this time. Despite this, its exceedingly simplistic design, and similarities to the Chinese flag, hold it back from scoring much higher.

153 - OMAN

Colour: 13   Design: 15

Identifiability: 19

Total: 47/100

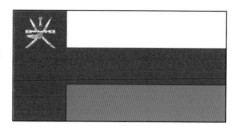

Oman's flag represents this nation fairly well, with the Omani emblem in the upper hoist side having represented their royal family since the 1700s, although without wanting to sound like a broken record, once again it is far too detailed to be featuring on a national flag. The red and green link the flag to those of many nearby nations with shared values, without the flags looking too similar that they could be confused with each other.

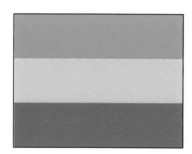

152 - GABON

Colour: 14   Design: 16

Identifiability: 18

Total: 48/100

The colour palette chosen for Gabon's flag is pleasing to the eye, representing the Gabonese landscape, for which they have become well known for. However, the flag does little more than this, and remains largely unknown to much of the rest of the world, suggesting that they may have benefitted from some more noteworthy imagery.

151 - SAN MARINO

Colour: 14   Design: 13

Identifiability: 21

Total: 48/100

The colour scheme is pleasant, but otherwise, the flag of San Marino is not one which has been thoughtfully or carefully designed, with a dominating coat of arms, and complete with unnecessary text. As one of Europe's smallest nations, it is likely that San Marino may have struggled to find meaningful imagery to use on their flag to depict their nation, but there must've been a better option than this.

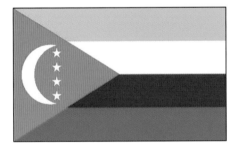

150 - COMOROS

Colour: 10   Design: 11

Identifiability: 28

Total: 49/100

The flag of this African island nation provides a good example of why flags should not typically contain more than 3 or 4 colours, because it results in a flag like this, which stands out from the crowd for all the wrong reasons. As a result, it becomes unclear what they were trying to convey about the Comoros, which is a real shame.

149 - TUVALU

Colour: 9   Design: 18

Identifiability: 22

Total: 49/100

Unlike many neighbouring countries in the Pacific Ocean, the flag of Tuvalu isn't particularly thoughtful in its design. As you may be able to guess, each star represents one of the islands of this small island nation, leading to a distinct lack of symmetry, not a necessity in flag design but with this flag it is notable. The Union Jack in the corner compounds this issue, and it would likely help this flag if Tuvalu opted for something more distinctly Tuvaluan.

148 - TONGA

Colour: 14   Design: 19

Identifiability: 16

Total: 49/100

In Tongan law, it states that under no circumstances can the flag of Tonga be changed or altered, and as such, the flag of Tonga has stood since it was first used in 1875. The flag isn't terrible but looks like a knock-off version of the older and more famous Swiss flag (47th), so I wonder if Tonga could have opted for something completely different.

147 - CAMEROON

Colour: 13   Design: 17

Identifiability: 19

Total: 49/100

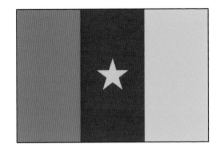

Again, much like many nearby countries in Western Africa, Cameroon has made use of the 'Pan-African' colours, these being red, yellow, and green, inspired by Ethiopia's flag (20th). Unlike similar flags however - and I accept that this is only a minor advantage for Cameroon's flag - but the yellow stripe isn't in the middle this time, making this flag easier to recognise than similar flags.

146 - VATICAN CITY

Colour: 10   Design: 8

Identifiability: 32

Total: 50/100

The world's smallest country (depending on your definition of country, that is) is represented by this lackluster flag. The most glaring issue here is surely the coat of arms featuring on the fly half, which is (once again) far too complex. In addition, the Vatican City is one of just two countries to have a completely square flag (the other being Switzerland in 47th), in an unusual act of defiance to flag convention which makes the flag stand out for all the wrong reasons.

145 - MOZAMBIQUE

Colour: 8   Design: 19

Identifiability: 23

Total: 50/100

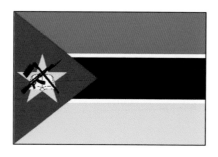

Speaking of flags that stand out for the wrong reasons, Mozambique's flag is likely one of the most bizarre instances of this, opting to depict among other objects an AK-47 (notably a *Russian* assault rifle, chosen for some inexplicable reason to represent Mozambique). Other than the mess of items in the flag's chevron, there are no glaring issues with the flag of Mozambique, and it certainly draws attention.

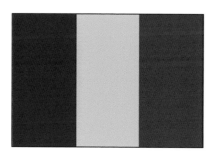

144 - CHAD

Colour: 15   Design: 16

Identifiability: 20

Total: 51/100

Those with a keen knowledge of flags may have already learned that the flags of Chad and Romania (75th) are the same as each other. Whilst this isn't *strictly* true (with slightly differing colour schemes), these similarities appear to be unintentional on both sides. Romania have used this flag earlier, although due to the use of the coat of arms on top of the tricolour during the communist era, during which Chad adopted their flag, Chad claim the sole rights to this flag. Although contentious, I have opted to back Romania in this debate.

143 - ERITREA

Colour: 8   Design: 19

Identifiability: 24

Total: 51/100

It is worth noting that by this stage in the list, each flag is scoring over 50/100, so they will all have at least some positive attributes associated with them. In the case of Eritrea, this flag is fairly unique, and the olive branches are a nice addition, albeit a bit on the complicated side.

142 - CHILE

Colour: 18   Design: 19

Identifiability: 15

Total: 52/100

Not a particularly bad flag however, unfortunately for Chile, their flag is noticeably similar to that of the 'Lone Star' state, Texas. Although the Chilean flag predates that of Texas, it cannot be denied that the confusion has caused difficulty in recognising their flag.

141 - PARAGUAY

Colour: 16   Design: 15

Identifiability: 21

Total: 52/100

Here's a fun fact: did you know that Paraguay's flag is the only national flag which officially has a reverse side which is different from the front side? You can look it up if you want, but as a prewarning - it is thoroughly disappointing, with the same design except for a different seal in the middle. Paraguay's flag may be notably different from many others in South America, but globally it is far from distinct, and the coat of arms doesn't do it any favours.

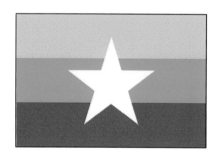

140 - MYANMAR

Colour: 12   Design: 21

Identifiability: 19

Total: 52/100

The flag of Myanmar, also known as Burma, besides from using similar colours to Lithuania (158th), is surprisingly unusual on the world stage, even with its relatively simple design. It is also relatively new, officially adopted in 2010, and was a major improvement from its previous flag. The symbolism behind this flag however is vague and predictable, so one would be unlikely to guess the country if they didn't already know this was the Myanmar flag.

139 -
MONTENEGRO

Colour: 6   Design: 17

Identifiability: 30

Total: 53/100

Montenegro, much like neighbouring Albania (33rd), has a flag which features a double-headed eagle, although clearly from the 26-point difference between the two flags, Montenegro could make use of this national symbol more effectively. Instead, Montenegro have excessively detailed their flag with their complex coat of arms, and the use of the gold border comes across as garish and over-the-top.

138 -
AFGHANISTAN

Colour: 12   Design: 15

Identifiability: 26

Total: 53/100

Despite changing their official flag more than any other country in the 20th century, Afghanistan still didn't seem to get the memo that less is often more. Instead, in their most recent change, Afghanistan opted to make their national emblem even bigger. The colours at least tell a story, of a troubled past and hope for the future.

137 - HONDURAS

Colour: 15   Design: 21

Identifiability: 18

Total: 54/100

Notably similar to the flags of nearby El Salvador and Nicaragua, the flag of Honduras also features blue and white horizontal stripes, although thankfully for Honduras, they opted for a considerably less complicated design than the coat of arms that its neighbours featured. The Honduran flag is still held back however by its overly basic design which could easily get mistaken for other flags.

136 - YEMEN

Colour: 14   Design: 20

Identifiability: 20

Total: 54/100

Many flags in the Middle East feature these colours, often alongside green, and these were initially intended to represent the different historical dynasties of the Arab world. These are a good tool when creating a flag in this part of the world, to give an obvious indication of the country it represents, although it should be designed considerately to distinguish it from other countries in the area. As a result, Yemen's more basic flag ranks in last place out of these nations.

135 - KOSOVO

Colour: 11   Design: 13

Identifiability: 30

Total: 54/100

Kosovo's flag depicts the outline of this partially recognised nation, under a curved row of six stars, said to represent the six main ethnic groups of Kosovo. As you will see with the flag of Cyprus on the next page, these are the only two nations in the world to use the outline of their country in their flag, which for the most part can be interpreted as a rather lazy way of depicting a country.

134 - TURKEY

Colour: 14   Design: 22

Identifiability: 18

Total: 54/100

Most will be able to recognise the flag of Turkey, thanks mostly to its longevity, as a flag which has been around in some form since the mid-19th century in the Ottoman Empire. The flag itself is rather simple, although it is worth appreciating that this flag was a bit of a trendsetter with regards to the star and crescent symbol. Since then, many more nations have used the star and crescent more effectively, making the Turkish flag seem overly simplistic.

133 - CYPRUS

Colour: 9   Design: 14

Identifiability: 32

Total: 55/100

Cyprus is one of two countries in this list whose flag depicts the outline of the country it represents (the other is Kosovo, as seen in 135th), and as demonstrated by many other countries in this list, there are clearly better and less convoluted ways of depicting your country. The olive branches however are a nice touch.

132 - TUNISIA

Colour: 14   Design: 23

Identifiability: 18

Total: 55/100

Tunisia's flag, notably very similar to the Turkish flag (134th) and even older, has been given a higher placement than the Turkish flag mainly because of the additional detail provided by placing the star and crescent in a white circle, a minor detail yet distinguishing this flag a little more. With that said, the Tunisian flag suffers the same lack of defining characteristics, a point which proves especially problematic when you consider the number of countries that went on to adopt the star and crescent in their own flags at a later date.

131 - BELARUS

Colour: 12   Design: 14

Identifiability: 29

Total: 55/100

The flag of Belarus suffers the same issue as Turkmenistan (183rd), although thankfully not to the same extent, however the pattern on the hoist side of the flag is far too detailed, no matter how representative it is of Belarusian culture.

130 - IRAQ

Colour: 14   Design: 23

Identifiability: 18

Total: 55/100

Much like many countries in the Arab world, Iraq makes use of the 'Pan-Arab' colours in their flag, helpfully illustrating to the viewer the part of the world this flag belongs to, and the shared history Iraq has with many of its neighbours. Much like neighbouring Saudi Arabia however, this flag unhelpfully attempts to distinguish itself through the use of text on the flag, lacking creativity or any sense of artistic flare.

129 - ARMENIA

Colour: 15   Design: 18

Identifiability: 22

Total: 55/100

The Armenian tricolour certainly stands out from other tricolour flags, thanks mostly to its use of orange, a surprisingly uncommon colour in vexillology. With that said, Armenians don't seem to be in agreement for what the colours actually represent, unfortunately holding this flag back from placing any higher on the list.

128 - SINGAPORE

Colour: 14   Design: 23

Identifiability: 18

Total: 55/100

Although very similar in design to the flag of nearby Indonesia (195th), the distinctive features of Singapore's flag mean it places far higher than its neighbour. The stars represent the core values of Singapore, and the moon illustrates that the nation is young and emerging. However, Singapore's flag is still clearly far from being unique, resulting in its placement in 128th.

127 - TOGO

Colour: 10   Design: 21

Identifiability: 24

Total: 55/100

This placement may be unpopular, so it is worth me reiterating that to place this high in the list, even though still in the bottom half, means this flag is still *fairly* good. The main issue comes from its design, which is essentially a rehashed version of the Liberian flag (38th), which itself was inspired by the U.S. flag. So, not particularly original, but Togo had the right idea.

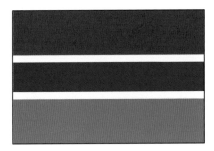

126 - THE GAMBIA

Colour: 12   Design: 24

Identifiability: 19

Total: 55/100

Perhaps the most redeeming quality of the flag of The Gambia is the imagery in its design. The geography of this African nation is a notable and defining characteristic, as a long, thin country essentially following part of the course of the Gambia river (from which it derives its name), and this is represented fairly well by the blue band in the middle, similar in shape to the country itself. However, this flag ranks in the bottom half, as it remains fairly indistinct and could easily be confused with many other flags.

125 - ZIMBABWE

Colour: 8   Design: 21

Identifiability: 27

Total: 56/100

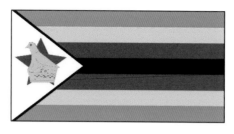

Zimbabwe's flag is certainly striking, but it cannot be denied that the flag looks very busy, with bold colours battling for the viewers' attention. The 'Zimbabwe Bird' that features in the chevron on the left is an effective symbol of the nation, but could have perhaps been better utilised, in a place where it could be the focal point.

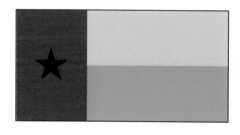

124 - GUINEA-BISSAU

Colour: 19   Design: 19

Identifiability: 18

Total: 56/100

The flag of this small African nation was inspired by that of Ghana (88th), essentially using all of the same components of Ghana's flag without looking too similar that they can't be distinguished from each other. The Bissau-Guinean flag features the 'Black Star of Africa' on the hoist side, a symbol intended by Ghana to represent the whole of Africa and unity among the nations, but has now become closely associated with Ghana more specifically, making Guinea-Bissau's flag somewhat harder to recognise.

123 - UNITED ARAB EMIRATES

Colour: 12   Design: 22

Identifiability: 22

Total: 56/100

Like a number of neighbouring countries, the United Arab Emirates uses the 'Pan-Arab' colours. This could have been utilised more effectively however, as the lack of detail or imagery means it can be easily confused for the flags of several other Arab states which similarly lack detail.

122 - CENTRAL AFRICAN REPUBLIC

Colour: 11   Design: 14

Identifiability: 32

Total: 57/100

Another flag placed firmly into the 'distinctive, but for the wrong reasons' category, the flag of the Central African Republic tries to illustrate far too much about the country in question, to the point where it is unnecessarily confusing and ends up achieving the opposite. At least it's colourful though.

121 - DOMINICAN REPUBLIC

Colour: 17   Design: 17

Identifiability: 23

Total: 57/100

The flag of the Dominican Republic is split into four quadrants by a white cross, an uncommon design for a country flag, although this unusual design is hindered by the extraordinarily complex emblem in the center, which is the national coat of arms. If you are willing to overlook this facet of its design however, this flag is well-designed, owing most of its identifiability to the alternating blue and red quadrants.

120 - MICRONESIA

Colour: 15   Design: 21

Identifiability: 21

Total: 57/100

Certainly one of the more underwhelming flags of Oceania, the flag of Micronesia depicts four stars, each representing one of the states of Micronesia. Not an especially interesting concept, but the end result is at least pleasant to look at, and the blue field effectively portrays that this is an island nation.

119 - SÃO TOMÉ AND PRÍNCIPE

Colour: 16   Design: 16

Identifiability: 25

Total: 57/100

The flag of São Tomé and Príncipe, one of Africa's smallest nations, does relatively well to represent one of the worlds lesser known countries through its design and use of colour. This flag uses the Pan-Africanist colours, providing a useful indication of where this nation is located, and the two stars unsurprisingly depict the separate islands of São Tomé and Príncipe. However, this flag would benefit massively from a more distinctive image or emblem to get itself noticed on the world stage.

118 - EGYPT

Colour: 10   Design: 23

Identifiability: 24

Total: 57/100

Egypt have set something of a trend amongst flags of the Middle East, being the first to use what have become known as the 'Arab Liberation' colours, an altered version (without green) of the Pan-Arab colours popular in the area. This flag was seen during the 1952 Egyptian Revolution, but without the emblem in the middle. The emblem was added 32 years later, and whilst overly complex for a flag, it does a good job distinguishing it from its neighbours.

117 - GRENADA

Colour: 16   Design: 17

Identifiability: 25

Total: 58/100

Grenada's flag is truly unlike any other, although the imagery represented here is rather difficult to interpret. For example, the small emblem on the hoist side, which may at first glance appear to be a flame, is in fact intended to depict a clove of nutmeg. Imagery like this would be ideal for a small nation such as Grenada, if it were executed more obviously, and this flag would rank higher if it didn't appear as chaotic as it does.

116 - SOMALIA

Colour: 14   Design: 19

Identifiability: 25

Total: 58/100

Although very simplistic, there is a unique charm to the flag of Somalia, with its bright and optimistic colours representing the Somali people in a positive light. Each of the points on the white star represents an area inhabited by the Somali people, and much like nearby Eritrea (143rd) and Djibouti (80th), Somalia is one of few nations in Northern Africa to adopt such light colours in their flag.

115 - NIGERIA

Colour: 14   Design: 20

Identifiability: 24

Total: 58/100

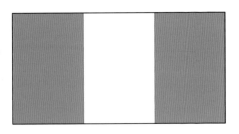

The flag of Nigeria is surprisingly unlike most other national flags, considering the basic design. The colour green has become widely associated with Nigeria, and so the use of a simple green and white design such as that seen in the Nigerian flag is more excusable that it would typically be. However, this flag would certainly still benefit from at least a little more detail.

114 - SERBIA

Colour: 16   Design: 19

Identifiability: 24

Total: 59/100

Serbia's flag uses red, white, and blue as well as a tricolour design, both especially common in Europe, although it is set apart by its coat of arms - a complicated design, but the double-headed eagle is objectively very cool. A simpler depiction of the Serbian eagle without the rest of the coat of arms would make this flag more recognisable without losing the meaning and depth behind the imagery here.

113 - CZECH REPUBLIC

Colour: 18   Design: 25

Identifiability: 16

Total: 59/100

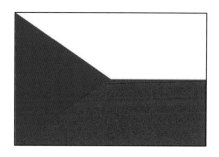

Despite its basic design and common colour scheme, the flag of the Czech Republic (now formally shortened to 'Czechia') is relatively recognisable, and has been in use for around a century, originating in the early days of Czechoslovakia. Before then, they used a plain red and white flag, exactly the same as the Polish flag (194th), to which they thankfully added a blue chevron to differentiate it. Red and white are colours historically associated with the region and with the Czechs, whilst blue was adopted to represent the Slovaks and other ethnic groups in the nation.

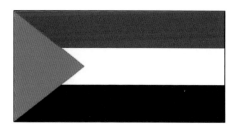

112 - SUDAN

Colour: 12   Design: 26

Identifiability: 21

Total: 59/100

Sudan's flag uses the 'Pan-Arab' colours along with many other nations in the Arab world, meaning that those with prior knowledge of similar flags will be able to guess that this flag represents a nearby nation. However, as should have become apparent with flags such as the UAE (123rd) and Iraq (130th), the main issue with many of these flags (including the Sudanese one) is often a lack of detail or defining characteristics, meaning that beyond the general area the country is located in, the viewer is given little information about Sudan specifically.

111 - THE NETHERLANDS

Colour: 18   Design: 16

Identifiability: 25

Total: 59/100

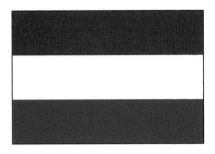

This is where things get a little contentious, as the Dutch flag is one of the oldest in the world still in use, adopted in the 1500s and influencing the design of the Russian (109th) and French (28th) flags. Why then does the Netherlands rank lower than the flags it inspired? For the most part, this relates to the influence of these flags, as the Dutch flag has been in use for a long time and influenced very few flags, whereas the Russian flag has influenced the designs of many of the Slavic nations, and the French flag was the first tricolour to start the trend of this design in national flags. This leaves the Netherlands with a very basic design, and little to show for it, since the flags it inspired did most of the hard work.

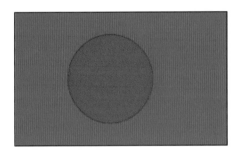

110 - BANGLADESH

Colour: 8   Design: 24

Identifiability: 28

Total: 60/100

On paper, the flag of Bangladesh should be far more likeable than it actually is. The disc on a plain background is a simple but unusual design that is used by just two other countries (Japan and Palau), however the symbolism is vague, and the red and green clash uncomfortably with each other.

109 - RUSSIA

Colour: 18   Design: 16

Identifiability: 26

Total: 60/100

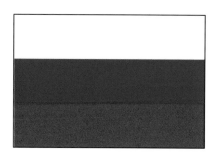

As discussed for the Netherlands (111th), the Russian flag was supposedly inspired by the Dutch flag, although the influence of the Russian flag appears to have reached far further, as the basis for the 'Pan-Slavic' colours seen in the flags of many Slavic countries such as Serbia (114th), Czechia (113th) and the Croatian flag below. This influence may be both a blessing and a curse, since it clearly means that many people have been paying attention to the Russian flag, although with the sheer number of other nations using the same colour scheme, the Russian flag becomes less recognisable.

108 - CROATIA

Colour: 17   Design: 25

Identifiability: 18

Total: 60/100

Croatia's flag is one which I suspect has become relatively well-known because of the national football team, with their kits adorning the chequered pattern seen in the coat of arms in the center of the Croatian flag. However, the shields above this pattern in the center are an unnecessary and complex detail, and without them I suspect the Croatian flag would rank far higher.

107 - LIBYA

Colour: 15   Design: 28

Identifiability: 17

Total: 60/100

Libya's flag is another example of using the 'Pan-Arab' colours popular in the area, although thankfully by this stage in the list, we are beginning to see these colours used more effectively. As previously established, a shared colour scheme can actually be very helpful for a flag, telling of shared values and history, although if these flags are too similar, this can understandably cause problems. In Libya's case however, the black bar unusually being in the middle means there is at least some distinction here. And yes, it is far better than their old flag, which was plain green.

106 - BHUTAN

Colour: 7   Design: 17

Identifiability: 37

Total: 61/100

The dragon that features in pride of place on the Bhutanese flag manages to be its most appealing feature and its major downfall. On one hand, the dragon serves as a strong mascot for the Dragon Kingdom's history and culture, not to mention how obviously cool it is. There is, however, clearly too much going on, and the dragons lack of colour makes the flag look unfinished.

105 - SIERRA LEONE

Colour: 17   Design: 20

Identifiability: 24

Total: 61/100

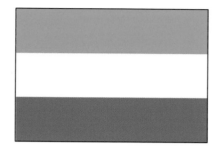

One of many tricolour flags in Western Africa, the flag of Sierra Leone differentiates itself with its more unusual colour scheme, with green representing the landscape and resources found here, white to depict justice and unity, and blue for its capital Freetown, which lies on the Atlantic coast. On a global scale, Sierra Leone's flag closely resembles the older but lesser known flag of the Galapagos Islands, a province in Ecuador, as well as having similarities to the flag of Uzbekistan (90th).

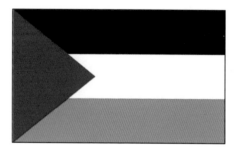

104 - PALESTINE

Colour: 12   Design: 26

Identifiability: 24

Total: 62/100

Another nation on this list using the Pan-Arab colours, the flag of Palestine uses these in a pleasant and simplistic manner, expressing the location and values of Palestine without any excessive or extravagant details. However, its remarkable similarity to the older Jordanian flag (94th), and a general lack of distinguishing imagery from many of the Pan-Arab flags, holds the Palestinian flag back from the top half of this list.

103 - SRI LANKA

Colour: 5   Design: 23

Identifiability: 34

Total: 62/100

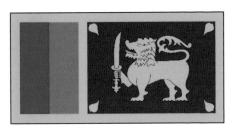

In a way, the chaotic and haphazard design of the Sri Lankan flag works in its favour, as it certainly isn't going to get confused with any other flags. Sri Lanka have ignored almost every convention in flag design, with an unusual colour scheme, a layout seen practically nowhere else, and far too much detail on the lion. The resultant product is at least a very memorable flag, albeit perhaps not the most pleasing to the eye. I applaud Sri Lanka's determination to stand out from the crowd though.

102 - CAMBODIA

Colour: 9   Design: 16

Identifiability: 37

Total: 62/100

The building depicted in the center is Angkor Wat, a temple in Cambodia, and one of Cambodia's most famous landmarks. The architecture here has become closely associated with Cambodia, and as such its inclusion in this flag was a decent idea, although evidently far too much detail has been added, holding back the Cambodian flag in the lower half of this list.

101 - KYRGYZSTAN

Colour: 13   Design: 27

Identifiability: 22

Total: 62/100

The creators of the flag of Kyrgyzstan (pronounced kur-gi-stan) had the right idea of having a large motif in the center of the flag, with little else to distract the viewers' attention, however they went a tad overboard when designing the sun in the middle. With that said, the concept of depicting the view of the roof from inside a traditional Kyrgyz yurt is a unique and appealing one.

100 - NEW ZEALAND

Colour: 16   Design: 18

Identifiability: 28

Total: 62/100

As most will be aware, New Zealand's flag is very similar to the Australian one (99th), with Australia's ultimately coming out on top. The two flags are often confused with each other, and although New Zealand's is older, Australia placed higher for two main reasons. The first is that both countries have been subject to campaigns to get their flags changed to far better and more unique options, although New Zealand's campaign got frustratingly close, and the *still* decided against it. The other, admittedly minor point is the unnecessary detail on the stars, making the flag appear a little too dark.

99 - AUSTRALIA

Colour: 17   Design: 18

Identifiability: 28

Total: 63/100

…and placing just above the flag of New Zealand is the similar Australian flag, subject to many of the same criticisms. Australia too has seen fierce debate regarding whether they should change their flag, although at no point yet has this looked as though it would actually happen. It is worth saying, although I didn't get chance to mention this for New Zealand's flag, that both designs have their benefits, for instance the Southern Cross hinting at the country's location. However, it remains that a more unique design with richer symbolism would be preferable.

98 - BRUNEI

Colour: 10   Design: 16

Identifiability: 37

Total: 63/100

At first sight, it can be hard to tell what Brunei's flag is trying to be, with much of the confusion owing to the national emblem in the middle. Whilst the flag breaks one of the most important rules by featuring text in the emblem, there is a strange likeability to Brunei's flag, and its unconventional design certainly makes the flag memorable.

97 - PALAU

Colour: 11   Design: 28

Identifiability: 24

Total: 63/100

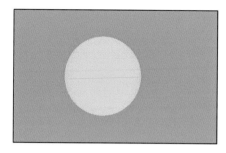

Palau's flag clearly isn't bad, but it is frustratingly 'safe', and is among some of the most simplistic national flags the world has to offer. The blue represents the Pacific Ocean, in which Palau is located, and the yellow represents the moon (not the sun, as you might expect).

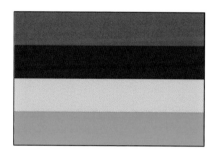

96 - MAURITIUS

Colour: 12   Design: 19

Identifiability: 32

Total: 63/100

Clearly not wanting to feel restricted by the standard tricolour, Mauritius has instead opted for a flag with four horizontal bars, proving in the process the importance of the 'rule of three' in flag design. With that said, the Mauritian flag stands out from the crowd, particularly impressive when you consider that it uses just plain block colours.

95 - URUGUAY

Colour: 16   Design: 29

Identifiability: 18

Total: 63/100

Uruguay's flag looks like the product of the flags of Argentina (77th) and Greece (54th) being merged together, providing a minor issue in terms of identifiability, however the 'Sun of May' in the canton serves as a good clue for the country it represents. The Sun of May is a symbol used in the flags of Uruguay and Argentina, said to represent the Incan sun god Inti.

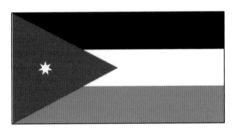

94 - JORDAN

Colour: 12   Design: 27

Identifiability: 25

Total: 64/100

Jordan's flag uses the Pan-Arab colours, now seen in many flags in the area, although it is worth noting that Jordan was very early to this trend, with many countries in the Arab world soon following suit. The flag was based on that of the Arab Revolt, and the colours were first adopted in 1921, with the current version adopted in 1928. Nowadays, it can be easily confused with the flags of nearby nations (especially Palestine, in 104th), so would benefit from more distinctive imagery.

93 - KUWAIT

Colour: 12   Design: 29

Identifiability: 23

Total: 64/100

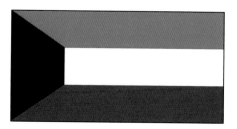

Another of the national flags using the Pan-Arab colours, there is little to be said about Kuwait's flag that hasn't already been said, other than mentioning the unique black trapezium on the left or 'hoist' side. There seemed to be little information available for why they chose this shape, but it has resulted in a more unusual and satisfying flag which is a little more distinctive than some of those nearby.

92 - GEORGIA

Colour: 14   Design: 24

Identifiability: 26

Total: 64/100

Georgia's flag (that is, Georgia the country, not Georgia the U.S. state) makes use of the St. George's cross, hence the similarity to the flag of England, and it is worth saying that both of these flags are incredibly old and historically significant to the areas in question. With that said, the St. George's cross had fallen out of use in Georgia for a long time, and was officially adopted as recently as 2004. As for the design, well, it's okay, and whilst distinctive in the local area, it gets lost on the world stage.

91 - AZERBAIJAN

Colour: 13 Design: 23

Identifiability: 28

Total: 64/100

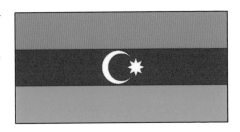

Azerbaijan's flag is another example of a tricolour done (relatively) well, with its most redeeming quality being the distinctive colour scheme it adorns, which is cultural significant, and unlikely to get confused with any other national flags. The star and crescent also tell of the country it represents and the dominant religion of Islam, without being overbearing or excessive in its design.

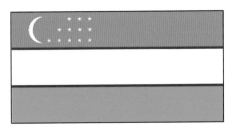

90 - UZBEKISTAN

Colour: 15 Design: 23

Identifiability: 26

Total: 64/100

The flag of Uzbekistan essentially functions as a tricolour, with the exceptions of the crescent and stars in the top left, and the red 'fimbriations' separating the stripes. These details add a unique edge to the Uzbek flag, helping it to stand out amongst similar flags such as that of Sierra Leone (105th). There are twelve stars on this flag, adopted for numerous reasons but partly due to the importance of the number twelve in Islam.

89 - MEXICO

Colour: 12   Design: 22

Identifiability: 30

Total: 64/100

Mexico's flag was amongst the first to adopt a tricolour design, with the same colours and a similar emblem first adopted in 1821, as Mexico gained independence from Spain. The colour scheme is evidently very similar to that of Italy (35th), with the Italian colours using slightly different shades and dating back even further, providing some competition for the recognisability of the Mexican flag. With that said, the coat of arms in the center of Mexico's flag is one of the more distinctive coat of arms used on a national level, based on a symbol used by the Aztecs, and depicting an eagle eating a serpent on top of a cactus.

88 - GHANA

Colour: 19   Design: 19

Identifiability: 26

Total: 64/100

Perhaps surprisingly low, it is worth saying that the Ghanaian flag has a lot of redeeming qualities, with a bold design rich in symbolism. It makes use of the 'Pan-African' colours of red, yellow, and green, which is both helpful for illustrating the part of the world this flag is from, and aesthetically pleasing too. It is this reliance on the colours chosen which is ultimately the main drawback of this flag however, as if one is going to make use of a popular colour set, they should consider more meaningful imagery than simply one star.

87 - SYRIA

Colour: 14   Design: 32

Identifiability: 19

Total: 65/100

The highest-ranking flag in this list to use the Pan-Arab colours, Syria's flag arguably makes the most effective use of this colour scheme, with the two stars in the middle distinguishing the Syrian flag from its neighbours relatively effectively whilst still suggesting the shared history they have. It is worth knowing however that the flag of Syria is disputed, with the Syrian opposition flying a tricolour flag of green, white, and black, with three red stars in the middle band, although for the sake of simplicity I have only ranked the flag of the current government.

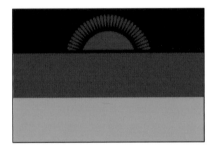

86 - MALAWI

Colour: 12   Design: 25

Identifiability: 28

Total: 65/100

The flag of Malawi was first adopted in 1964, but was subject to a temporary change between 2010 and 2012 when the government at the time made an unpopular decision to reorder the stripes and place a full white sun in the middle. The flag was then officially changed back to the previous design, featuring a sun with 31 rays to illustrate that Malawi was the 31st independent African nation. This flag features the Pan-African colours, and its relatively distinctive design gets it noticed on the world stage.

85 - ECUADOR

Colour: 16   Design: 18

Identifiability: 31

Total: 65/100

The flags of Ecuador, Colombia and Venezuela all bear the same colour scheme, which serves as a helpful illustration of the part of the world these flags represent, and each flag has a different feature to differentiate it from its neighbours. With a large and overly detailed coat of arms at pride of place, the flag of Ecuador doesn't quite live up to the standards of its counterparts, however the colour scheme remains its saving grace.

84 - BAHRAIN

Colour: 14   Design: 24

Identifiability: 28

Total: 66/100

As you will see from the next two placements, the flags of Bahrain and Qatar are very similar, with the Qatari flag ultimately coming out on top. The lower placement of Bahrain's flag is due mostly to its more basic and predictable design, and that it was adopted after that of Qatar, although admittedly there isn't much between these flags. The design of these flags is unlike anything seen anywhere else in the world, although in the case of Bahrain, the meaning behind this design is unclear.

83 - QATAR

Colour: 9   Design: 25

Identifiability: 32

Total: 66/100

As just stated for Bahrain (84th), Qatar's flag is remarkably similar to that of this nearby nation. Interestingly however, Qatar's flag is the only flag to have a ratio longer than 2:1, making it the longest national flag. It was also initially intended to be red like Bahrain's flag, yet it is reported that due to the quality of the dye used, it faded in the harsh heat, with the resultant maroon colour eventually made official. The more unique design and backstory places Qatar's flag above Bahrain's.

82 - SLOVENIA

Colour: 17   Design: 26

Identifiability: 23

Total: 66/100

There is seemingly little to say about the flag of Slovenia, other than its similarity to many other flags of Eastern Europe, and in particular, the similarly named but very distinct nation of Slovakia (43rd). Slovenia's flag is often somewhat erroneously described as using the 'Pan-Slavic' colours popularised by Russia, as although they use the same colour scheme, this is in fact derived from the historical colours associated with the Duchy of Carniola (situated in present day Slovenia).

81 - INDIA

Colour: 11   Design: 24

Identifiability: 31

Total: 66/100

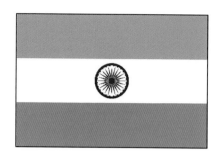

I suspect that India's flag is well-known mostly because India itself is relatively familiar to most people, however the emblem in the middle helps make this design recognisable. The emblem, a wheel with 24 spokes known as the Ashoka Chakra, represents the law of Dharma, an important concept in Indian religions such as Hinduism and Buddhism. This flag was adopted in the 1940s around the time of Indian independence, and is reminiscent of the previous design used by the independence movement, which bore a spinning wheel as proposed by Gandhi.

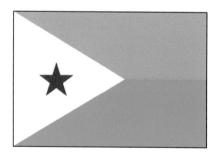

80 - DJIBOUTI

Colour: 16   Design: 26

Identifiability: 24

Total: 66/100

The flag of Djibouti, situated on the East coast of Africa, has a light and optimistic appearance, but with a red star to honour those who lost their lives during the establishment of Djibouti. These bright colours (especially the light blue) are unusual for North Africa, although shared by bordering Somalia (116th) and Eritrea (143rd), providing a useful link between these flags and aiding their identifiability.

79 - PAKISTAN

Colour: 14   Design: 24

Identifiability: 28

Total: 66/100

The flag of Pakistan depicts an off-center star and crescent, much like many other national flags, although remains distinctive despite its simple design because of the white bar on the hoist side, and the relatively uncommon green and white colour scheme. The colours are both said to represent the country's religious groups, with the green depicting the Muslim majority, and white to represent the minority religious groups. Pakistan's flag may not be the most exciting to look at, but functions well in representing this country.

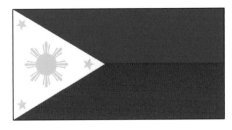

78 - PHILIPPINES

Colour: 17   Design: 26

Identifiability: 23

Total: 66/100

The flag of the Philippines has a little-known but fascinating fact associated with it, being that in times of war, it is flow upside-down - a feature of which the Philippines is the only nation to officially adopt (some other nations may fly their flags upside-down to indicate a state of crisis). The flag is generally pleasing to the eye, but the sun on the hoist side is unnecessarily intricate.

77 - ARGENTINA

Colour: 16   Design: 31

Identifiability: 19

Total: 66/100

Much like neighbouring Uruguay (95th), Argentina's flag features the 'Sun of May' emblem, said to represent the Incan sun god Inti. The more simplistic design in the Argentinian flag however provides less distraction and diverts the viewers' attention to this emblem, unique to the area, helping this flag to be more easily identified.

76 - PANAMA

Colour: 17   Design: 26

Identifiability: 23

Total: 66/100

The Panamanian flag has a unique and memorable design without trying too hard to get itself noticed or using any excessive imagery, hence the relatively high score for design. However, the symbolism behind this design is a little scant, serving to represent the two main political parties in Panama, and peace between them, when it feels as though they missed an opportunity to depict something more distinctively Panamanian.

75 - ROMANIA

Colour: 15   Design: 26

Identifiability: 26

Total: 67/100

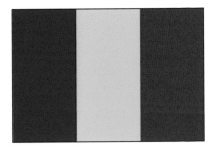

As discussed earlier for Chad's flag (144th), the flags of Chad and Romania are almost exactly the same, so why the massive difference in rankings? Put simply, Romania was one of the first countries in the world to officially adopt a tricolour, a few decades after France, and is steeped in historical significance for Romania. Without wishing to take sides in international affairs, it is hard to understand how Chad has a claim to these colours, just because Romania had a coat of arms over the tricolour at some point.

74 - EAST TIMOR

Colour: 16   Design: 26

Identifiability: 25

Total: 67/100

The flag of East Timor, or Timor-Leste (whose name translates as 'East East'), has a unique and appealing design with two differently sized chevrons on the hoist side adding an unusual sense of perspective without trying too hard. With that said, although thoughtfully crafted, the flag has little in terms of unique symbolism behind its design. The red represents the suffering of the East Timorese, yellow for the fight for independence, black for the colonial history, and a white star for the future hopes of East Timor.

73 - COLOMBIA

Colour: 16   Design: 21

Identifiability: 30

Total: 67/100

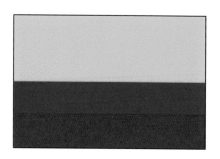

Colombia is one of three South American countries whose flag is a tricolour of yellow, blue, and red (along with Ecuador and Venezuela), taken from the flag of the historical country of Gran Colombia, in which these countries are located. Out of these three countries, Colombia places 2nd, as there are no major issues with the design (like a large coat of arms), but the flag does little to distinguish itself from its neighbours. In general, this shared colour scheme is a helpful way of illustrating the shared history these countries have, but to maximise how effective this is, each nation should have some distinctive imagery on their flag, which Colombia unfortunately does not.

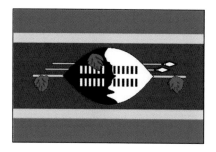

72 - ESWATINI

Colour: 10   Design: 24

Identifiability: 33

Total: 67/100

Eswatini, formerly known as Swaziland, is represented by this meaningful yet complex design depicting a traditional Nguni shield and staff, alongside two spears. The Nguni people, an umbrella term including the Swazi and Zulu people, make up the majority of Eswatini, and the black and white colour on the shield is said to represent the harmony between the different ethnic groups of this nation.

71 - NAMIBIA

Colour: 14   Design: 29

Identifiability: 25

Total: 68/100

Perhaps one of the most appealing aspects of the Namibian flag is the representation of the Atlantic coast in blue and the landscape in green, which is a concept shared with Tanzania (42nd) on the Indian Ocean coast (these countries do not border each other, but nonetheless there is a charm from these two Southern African nations sharing this concept). There is a certain childish quality to this flag with the depiction of the sun in the top left, but the symbolism behind this flag is still very thoughtful.

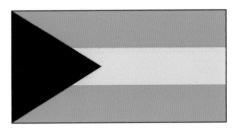

70 - BAHAMAS

Colour: 17   Design: 22

Identifiability: 30

Total: 69/100

The main selling point of the Bahamian flag is its colour scheme, with a distinct and obvious Caribbean feel to it. With a pleasant design and no obvious flaws, the flag of the Bahamas lands itself in the top half of this list, although it would certainly benefit from something more explicitly Bahamian to differentiate itself from other island nations, and to celebrate their own unique culture.

69 -
KAZAKHSTAN

Colour: 11   Design: 28

Identifiability: 30

Total: 69/100

Despite the intricacy of parts of this flag, Kazakhstan's flag is notably pleasant to look at, depicting an eagle in flight and making use of culturally important imagery and colour for the Kazakhs. The pattern on the hoist side is known as the 'koshkar muiz' or 'horn of the ram', also holding meaning for the Kazakh population, but is perhaps excessively detailed for a national flag.

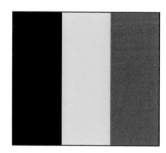

68 - BELGIUM

Colour: 19   Design: 20

Identifiability: 30

Total: 69/100

The Belgian flag has an unusual shape, officially with the proportions of 13:15, making it one of the squarer national flags (however, a more standard 2:3 ratio is often flown). A minor issue, but this defiance of flag convention is a tad frustrating when flown alongside other national flags. More well known however are the similarities to the German flag (13th), which uses similar colours and has arguably become more recognisable. Still a good choice of flag by Belgium, but somewhat overshadowed by that of its neighbour.

67 - PORTUGAL

Colour: 10   Design: 21

Identifiability: 38

Total: 69/100

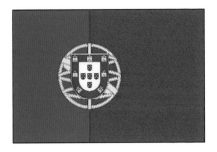

Portugal's flag will be familiar to most, thanks partly to the distinctive colour scheme used, which I suspect owes a lot of its recognition to the kit of the Portuguese national football team. The flag features a simplified version of the still rather complex national coat of arms however, hence the lower score for the 'Design' category.

66 - CHINA

Colour: 12   Design: 23

Identifiability: 35

Total: 70/100

China's flag is, if anything, a little underwhelming, with its basic colour scheme and imagery, yet nonetheless it has become an effective symbol of China. The official Chinese interpretation of the symbolism behind their flag has changed over time, particularly with relation to the stars, although it is generally agreed upon that they represent the unity of the Chinese people under a single party state.

65 - KIRIBATI

Colour: 9   Design: 29

Identifiability: 32

Total: 70/100

The flag of Kiribati (pronounced kiri-bas) provides an obvious depiction of the kind of country Kiribati is, that is, a small nation in the Pacific Ocean. The flag is undeniably cool, yet it also cannot be denied that the colour scheme and design come across as lurid and garish. In particular, the flag is a little overly detailed, and I could find no obvious reason for the red colour of the sky, which feels unfitting. Despite this, there remains a tangible charm about the Kiribati flag, and a certain likeable quality that few flags manage to achieve.

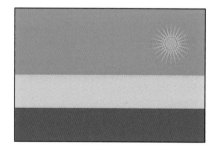

64 - RWANDA

Colour: 14   Design: 27

Identifiability: 29

Total: 70/100

Rwanda's flag was adopted in 2001 as a significant departure from their previous design, as this has come to be associated with the Rwandan genocide of the previous decade, and as such, this new design is one which focusses on themes of unity and the future. The flag expresses these themes clearly, as well as depicting the vibrant landscape that Rwanda offers.

63 - THAILAND

Colour: 18 Design: 29

Identifiability: 23

Total: 70/100

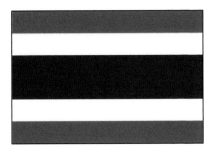

Finding a winner between the flags of Thailand and Costa Rica (62nd) was a challenging task, with the flags being practically identical except for the blue and red swapping places, however as the younger flag, Thailand ended up placing 2nd out of the two. Besides from Costa Rica's flag however, the flag of Thailand is a simplistic but surprisingly unique and satisfying flag, worthy of a place in the top half of this list.

62 - COSTA RICA

Colour: 18   Design: 29

Identifiability: 24

Total: 71/100

As just discussed with the flag of Thailand (63rd), these two have very similar flags, yet which are surprisingly unusual amongst other countries. Little more can be said for this flag which hasn't already been said for Thailand, but Costa Rica's flag is a refreshing sight amongst a host of Central American flags which look frustratingly similar to each other.

61 - JAPAN

Colour: 14   Design: 26

Identifiability: 31

Total: 71/100

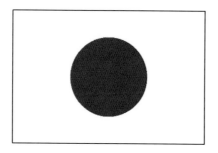

Japan's flag is widely recognised, although I suspect this is thanks mostly to Japan being a well-known country. The flag design is different to most, but about as basic as it gets, with the common red and white colour scheme not helping the situation. However, the flag has been in use for well over a century, and links well to the nickname of Japan as the 'Land of the Rising Sun', so credit where it's due, this is still a good flag and a strong representation of Japan.

60 - LESOTHO

Colour: 16   Design: 29

Identifiability: 26

Total: 71/100

The flag of Lesotho, a nation surrounded completely by South Africa, most notably features a Basotho hat called a 'mokorotlo' in the center, serving as a relatively good example of meaningful symbolism being expressed in a simplistic and appealing way. The colour scheme used is unusual too, further differentiating the flag of Lesotho from those of other nations.

59 - SURINAME

Colour: 18   Design: 34

Identifiability: 19

Total: 71/100

Possible one of the most aesthetically pleasing flags of the entire world, the flag of this South American nation has been carefully and thoughtfully crafted to be distinct without an over-the-top design. The main drawback of this flag would be the 'Identifiability' category, as it is not particularly clear what is being represented here, with few visual clues to the part of the world this country is in, or what it is known for.

58 - FINLAND

Colour: 14   Design: 28

Identifiability: 30

Total: 72/100

Finland is the lowest ranking of the five nations bearing the Nordic cross, yet still makes it to the top 60. As will become apparent with the other Nordic nations in this list, the Nordic cross design is one of the best and most effective simple designs seen in vexillology, clearly illustrating the shared history of these nations whilst giving room to express the uniqueness of the specific country through colour. Finland's flag ranks lowest as one of the lesser known and more basic applications of this design, although it is still a great flag.

57 - MALAYSIA

Colour: 16   Design: 29

Identifiability: 28

Total: 73/100

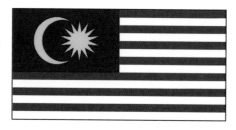

Malaysia's flag is clearly very similar to that of the U.S., although it is worth noting that the symbolism behind the Malaysian flag is significant and justifies such a similar design being adopted many years after the U.S. flag. The design essentially merges two preexisting flags from the area, the Majapahit flag (where Indonesia's red and white colour scheme is inspired from), and the flag of Johor. The resultant flag is one which evidently has themes in common with other flags (not only the U.S. but Liberia too in 38th) but is distinctive enough not to get confused with them, and is rich in meaning and history.

56 - UGANDA

Colour: 16   Design: 22

Identifiability: 35

Total: 73/100

I would assume that many reading this book will have a wide range of opinions on the Ugandan flag, depending on the aspect of this flag you are drawn to. On one hand, the colours used are bold and make this flag very memorable, particularly since it has almost nothing in common with other East African flags. However, the repetition of these colours, and the white circle depicting a crane in the center, contribute to a rather erratic flag design.

55 - ALGERIA

Colour: 14   Design: 28

Identifiability: 32

Total: 74/100

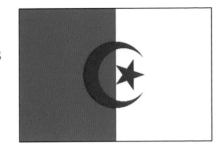

Despite the star and crescent appearing in many other national flags, Algeria have managed to design one which is widely recognisable, with the green and white field helping to differentiate it from other such flags. As such, Algeria have demonstrated that frequently used imagery, if relevant to the culture and beliefs of many in a given nation, can still be effectively used.

54 - GREECE

Colour: 15   Design: 25

Identifiability: 34

Total: 74/100

The Greek flag is one which is shrouded in legend, dating back to 1822 and with a number of theories for what the blue and white stripes represent, although the prevailing consensus seems as though they represent the syllables in the phrase 'Elefthería í Thánatos', or 'Freedom or Death'. This phrase saw use when the Greeks were declaring independence from the Ottoman Empire, and has since been adopted as the country's official motto. The colours and cross highlight the Greek Orthodox church, and have also come to be associated with the sea and architecture for which Greece is known.

53 - TAJIKISTAN

Colour: 14   Design: 33

Identifiability: 27

Total: 74/100

Tajikistan's flag consists of a triband of red, white, and green, much like the flag of Hungary (160th), and if it were left like this, it would certainly not have ranked so highly. Many outside of the area may not know very much about Tajikistan, but the unusual crown emblem in the middle makes this flag more notable and recognisable, representing the Tajik people through the links to the Persian word for crown 'tâj'.

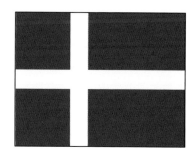

52 - DENMARK

Colour: 13   Design: 28

Identifiability: 33

Total: 74/100

The Danish flag holds the world record as the oldest national flag in continual use, and is one which is steeped in legend, and so the historical significance of this flag is immense. In addition, the Nordic cross is a great feature of the Nordic countries, showing the shared history of the countries whilst allowing each to express themselves uniquely through the colours used. One could argue however that this flag is somewhat too simplistic.

51 - CUBA

Colour: 18   Design: 34

Identifiability: 22

Total: 74/100

The flag of Cuba has an appealing design, although it is not without its challenges, most clearly seen in its similarities with the flag of the nearby U.S. territory Puerto Rico. Cuba's flag predates Puerto Rico's, and in fact, Puerto Rico's flag was specifically inspired by Cuba's, first adopted by an independence movement that had links to Cuba. Whilst this may provide some difficulty in identifying the Cuban flag, the eye-catching design helps bring Cuba's total score up.

50 - SOLOMON ISLANDS

Colour: 12   Design: 31

Identifiability: 31

Total: 74/100

The Solomon Islands, a set of islands in the Pacific Ocean, is represented by this distinctive design, with imagery that is fairly easy to interpret. The blue represents water, the green represents land and vegetation, and the yellow represents the sun, all combining to conjure up images of the tropical landscape of these islands. The stars were initially intended to depict the five provinces of the Solomon Islands, although since then, this number has risen to nine, with the flag remaining the same.

49 - SPAIN

Colour: 13   Design: 21

Identifiability: 40

Total: 74/100

The Spanish flag is widely recognised, with the colours red and yellow being closely linked to the country, although would be improved by having a more simplistic depiction of their coat of arms. The flag dates back to 1785 as a naval flag or 'ensign', but in the following two centuries underwent numerous changes, including the flag of the Second Spanish Republic, which unusually featured the colour purple (a colour nowadays used by just two national flags, Nicaragua in 166th and Dominica in 161st).

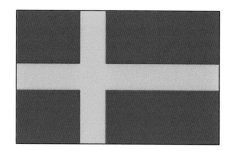

48 - SWEDEN

Colour: 15   Design: 28

Identifiability: 31

Total: 74/100

Coming in 3rd place out of the 5 that feature the Nordic cross, Sweden's flag should not be overlooked, and serves as an example of how the colours used by a country's flag can become one of the first things that one thinks of when considering that country. The flag is perhaps, however, a little too simplistic, and may have benefitted from outlines (or 'fimbriations') around the Nordic cross as seen in the flags of Norway and Iceland.

47 - SWITZERLAND

Colour: 14   Design: 29

Identifiability: 32

Total: 75/100

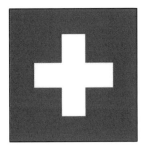

As Roger Federer supposedly responded in an interview when asked about life in Switzerland, "the flag is a big plus". Whilst the veracity of this quote is questionable, the Swiss flag has a simple and recognisable flag, surprisingly dissimilar to any other national flag. With that said, it is one of just two national flags that are completely square (the other being the Vatican City in 146th), and as discussed there, these flags have little reason to defer from normal flag convention.

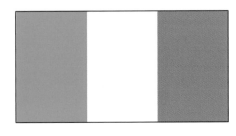

46 - IRELAND

Colour: 15   Design: 28

Identifiability: 32

Total: 75/100

The Irish flag has been used officially since 1916, although historically it dates back to the 1840s, presented as an act of solidarity by some French citizens, making the Irish flag one of the oldest tricolours in the world. It is notably similar to the flag of the Ivory Coast (176th), although with a different aspect ratio and the green and orange swapping places, but with the Irish flag being significantly older, the Ivorian flag has ranked far lower as they should've considered these similarities.

45 - MONGOLIA

Colour: 8   Design: 29

Identifiability: 38

Total: 75/100

The Mongolian flag most notably features the 'Soyombo' symbol on the hoist side, a very important cultural symbol of Mongolia with its origins in Buddhism. The symbol is also seen in Mongolia's national emblem, a more complex design than that which features on the flag, thankfully. This makes it a fantastic symbol to use in representing Mongolia, in a flag deserving of a place in the top quarter of this list.

44 - VENEZUELA

Colour: 16   Design: 27

Identifiability: 32

Total: 75/100

Much like its neighbours Colombia (73rd) and Ecuador (85th), the flag of Venezuela uses yellow, blue, and red, in a useful illustration to the viewer of their shared history as previous constituents of the nation of Gran Colombia. Out of these three flags, Venezuela ranks the highest, as it is the only one to use basic imagery (in the form of eight stars) to distinguish it from these similar flags. The eight stars represent the provinces of Venezuela when Guayana joined the newly independent nation in the early 19th century, although nowadays Venezuela no longer has provinces but instead 23 states and a capital district.

43 - SLOVAKIA

Colour: 18   Design: 34

Identifiability: 24

Total: 76/100

Slovakia's flag is a very rare example of a national flag featuring the national coat of arms and looking *better* as a result. Whilst typically, a nations coat of arms is extremely intricate and features plenty of lavish details, the Slovak coat of arms is very simple, so there was no need to simplify the coat of arms when depicting it on this flag. Not only this, but given the common colours chosen (particularly frequent in the Slavic nations of Eastern Europe), this emblem provides the necessary detail to differentiate the Slovak flag from those of its neighbours. Certainly one of the most overlooked flags of Europe.

42 - TANZANIA

Colour: 12   Design: 33

Identifiability: 31

Total: 76/100

The diagonal stripes adopted in the flag of Tanzania, along with several other nations featuring in the top half of this list, is one of the most distinctive of the more basic designs seen amongst national flags. Tanzania's is no exception, portraying the natural landscape and resources, the people, and the coastline on the Indian Ocean in an appealing way.

41 - IRAN

Colour: 18   Design: 29

Identifiability: 30

Total: 77/100

The Iranian flag is a good example of striking the right balance between simplicity and detail, and features Iran's national emblem in the middle of the white bar. On either side of the white bar is a stylised version of the 'takbir', a phrase common in Islam meaning 'God is the greatest'. In this sense, Iran's flag is the exception that proves the rule that flags should not have any text of writing on them, since this adjusted version of the Kufic script in Arabic is not too complex or distracting, and adds some welcomed decorative detail.

40 - LEBANON

Colour: 15   Design: 31

Identifiability: 31

Total: 77/100

The flag of Lebanon is worthy of a place in the top quarter of this list, thanks mostly to the symbol or 'charge' of a cedar of Lebanon in the center of the flag. It is a good example of using a relatively simple icon that has a close cultural connection to the country in question, although evidently the cedar tree is still a little detailed, and would be difficult to recall precisely from memory.

39 - NEPAL

Colour: 8   Design: 30

Identifiability: 40

Total: 78/100

Let's be clear - wherever the flag of Nepal places on this list, it is bound to frustrate some people. On the world stage, Nepal's flag sticks out like a sore thumb, as the only national flag to have more than 4 sides, and whilst I would generally prefer for countries to stick to rectangular flags with a ratio of 2:1, Nepal's flag may just be the exception to prove the rule. That said, if you overlook the unique shape, Nepal's flag isn't particularly interesting, keeping it from the higher positions on this list.

38 - LIBERIA

Colour: 18   Design: 32

Identifiability: 28

Total: 78/100

At first glance, Liberia's flag may appear to be a mere knockoff of the U.S. flag, however when you consider the unique history of Liberia as a nation of freed slaves from the U.S. in the 19th century, Liberia's flag begins to tell more of a story. It is distinct enough not to get confused with the U.S. flag itself and stands out amongst the flags of Africa. Liberia's county flags are not due the same such praise however...

37 - ST. VINCENT AND THE GRENADINES

Colour: 13 Design: 36

Identifiability: 29

Total: 78/100

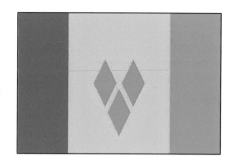

The flag of Saint Vincent and the Grenadines features three green diamonds, referring to their title as the 'Jewels of the Caribbean', with the 'v' formation in which they are laid out subtly hinting to the nations name. This is one of the few examples in this list of a nation *finally* replacing a design which featured their coat of arms, an unnecessary and complex design which they replaced in 1985 whilst keeping the same general colour scheme.

36 - NORTH MACEDONIA

Colour: 13 Design: 31

Identifiability: 34

Total: 78/100

North Macedonia's flag features a basic but appealing design based on the sun, and looks unlike any other national flag. This is based on a national symbol of Macedonia, and although this symbol may not be widely known, it has resulted in a very likeable flag design. Also, if you don't recall the 'North' in North Macedonia, this was officially added to the nations name recently after a dispute with neighbouring Greece, who claimed this caused confusion with the Greek region of Macedonia.

35 - ITALY

Colour: 18   Design: 28

Identifiability: 32

Total: 78/100

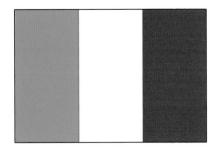

Whilst perhaps not the most interesting flag, the Italian tricolour is rich in history, inspired directly by the French flag, and with evidence of these colours in use as far back as the late 1700s. Since then, green, white, and red have become closely linked to Italy, meaning that even this simple design has been a key factor in shaping Italian identity. Italy's flag has undergone various changes since these colours were first used, with the current iteration adopted in 1946.

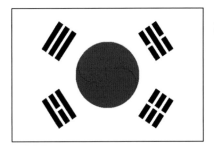

34 - SOUTH KOREA

Colour: 7   Design: 31

Identifiability: 40

Total: 78/100

One of the most well-known and recognisable flags in the world, the flag of South Korea is unlike any other national flag in its design. The Taegeuk in the center, deriving from the yin-yang symbol, represents the balance present in the universe and is found in various religions in South Korea. Surrounding this are four trigrams, said to represent various concepts including the four seasons and four cardinal directions, and are again important symbols in various religious traditions. The design may be a little complex, but it has an undeniable and unique appeal.

33 - ALBANIA

Colour: 14   Design: 32

Identifiability: 33

Total: 79/100

The Albanian flag is undeniably hardcore, in black and red and sporting a double-headed eagle, a symbol which has been associated with Albania for centuries. The main advantage of Albania's flag is simply how eye-catching and striking its design is, unlikely to get overlooked or confused with any other flags. At the same time, the double-headed eagle also provides the flags main weakness, as recalling this motif precisely from memory would be a challenge to say the least.

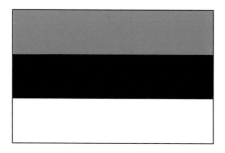

32 - ESTONIA

Colour: 20   Design: 30

Identifiability: 29

Total: 79/100

One of the highest-ranking plain tricolour flags in this list, the flag of Estonia is a prime example of what can be achieved using this relatively simple design. Estonia's flag is often said to depict the harsh, frosty landscape of this Baltic nation, leading to a flag with meaningful symbolism, and which stands out amongst other tricolours.

31 - BOTSWANA

Colour: 18   Design: 32

Identifiability: 30

Total: 80/100

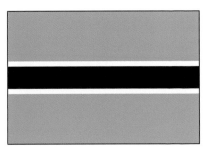

The flag of Botswana stands out from the crowd when you consider those of its neighbours in Africa, using a very different colour palette. Botswana's flag, unusually for the continent, remains neutral to the country's political standpoint, and instead reflects its natural resources and the harmony between its people. It may not be the most interesting flag, but it is a good example that sometimes, less is more.

30 - ST. KITTS AND NEVIS

Colour: 16   Design: 34

Identifiability: 30

Total: 80/100

The flag of the Caribbean nation of St. Kitts and Nevis strikes a great balance between simplicity and a unique design, resulting in one of the most thoughtful flag designs even by Caribbean standards. The symbolism too is relatively easy to interpret, with green for the nation's vibrant terrain, red for their struggle against colonialism, yellow for the tropical weather, and black for its people's African heritage. The two stars in the center stripe unsurprisingly depict the two islands of St. Kitts (formally known as St. Christopher) and Nevis, but are also said to stand for hope and liberty.

29 - TRINIDAD AND TOBAGO

Colour: 15   Design: 33

Identifiability: 32

Total: 80/100

Despite the relatively small size of this nation, many may still recognise the flag of Trinidad and Tobago, not least because it seems to effectively embody the passion and dynamism of this Caribbean nation. Trinidad and Tobago's flag is said to represent earth (black), water (white) and fire (red). Whilst this may not be immediately clear, it is hard not to see the charm in the imagery represented here, telling of two nations separated by the sea by nonetheless united.

28 - FRANCE

Colour: 18   Design: 28

Identifiability: 34

Total: 80/100

The flag of France is (arguably) the original tricolour, often referred to as just 'the tricolour', and should be given credit for this, hence the high placement. The tricolour has its roots in the French Revolution, and has gone on to inspire practically every tricolour flag since then. The basic choice of design and colour, however influential, hold this flag back from scoring any higher, although a reasonable claim could be made that the French flag is the most significant throughout history.

27 - CAPE VERDE

Colour: 17   Design: 30

Identifiability: 35

Total: 82/100

Cape Verde (or Cabo Verde as it is referred to for diplomatic purposes) is an island nation lying off the West coast of Africa, as depicted by the ten stars, each representing one of the main islands. The flag is clearly very similar to that used by the European Union, although the white and red stripes make it distinct enough for this not to cause issues. A great showing from Cape Verde, representing their nation with this unique and memorable flag.

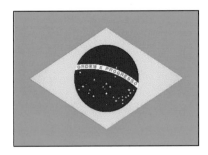

26 - BRAZIL

Colour: 18   Design: 24

Identifiability: 40

Total: 82/100

Few flags are as immediately identifiable as that of Brazil, and it has become a strong and impactful symbol of this diverse nation. The colour scheme in particular is very effective, as although not the initial intention, it brings home thoughts of the verdant landscape of the Amazon rainforest and the beaches of Brazil's coastal cities. There is one major issue with the Brazilian flag - it commits the cardinal sin of having unnecessary text, and at the center of attention at that.

25 - ICELAND

Colour: 18   Design: 34

Identifiability: 30

Total: 82/100

Another flag using the Nordic cross, and another flag proving why this is such a strong design. The cross itself represents Christianity, and has been in use amongst the Nordic nations for hundreds of years, although the flag of Iceland was adopted far more recently in the 20th century alongside the founding of a republic. As a design, it is straightforward and pleasing to the eye, and gives each nation that uses it a fair amount of room to differentiate their flag through the use of colour.

24 - UNITED STATES

Colour: 18   Design: 25

Identifiability: 40

Total: 83/100

The U.S. flag or 'star-spangled banner' is among the most well-known and iconic flags of the world, thanks in part to its unique design, rich meaning, and depth, of which there seems to be something inherently appealing. However, the decision to represent each state with a star feels like it backfired on this flag when the number of states rose to 50, and as an American friend pointed out to me once, drawing out all 50 stars for a school project soon becomes a chore. Otherwise, a good showing from the U.S.

23 - NORWAY

Colour: 18   Design: 34

Identifiability: 31

Total: 83/100

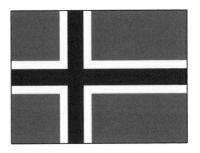

The highest ranking of the flags with the Nordic cross, Norway's flag ranks higher that the similar Icelandic flag (25th) mostly because it predates it, with the Norwegian flag dating back to the early 19th century. The Nordic cross is shared by the five independent Nordic nations, each using different colour combinations, and is an effective symbol of the countries shared heritage. Only Norway and Iceland however feature a white outline (or 'fimbriation') around the cross, adding much-needed detail.

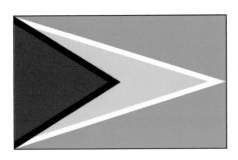

22 - GUYANA

Colour: 18   Design: 32

Identifiability: 33

Total: 83/100

The national flag of Guyana was adopted in 1966 when they gained independence from the UK, and is of particular interest, as it was designed by the late vexillologist Whitney Smith, one of the leading figures in flag study and even pioneering the term 'vexillology' itself. It is easy to see the influence of an expert in the field here, as the Guyanese flag has an unusual and memorable design without an unnecessary or convoluted imagery.

21 - CANADA

Colour: 16   Design: 32

Identifiability: 35

Total: 83/100

One of the most regularly cited examples of quality flag design, Canada have nailed the imagery in their flag, with the maple leaf serving as a simple but instantly recognisable symbol closely associated with the country it represents. The colours chosen are pleasing to the eye, although 'played out' a bit, with this colour combination appearing very frequently in the flags of the world.

20 - ETHIOPIA

Colour: 14   Design: 37

Identifiability: 32

Total: 83/100

The Ethiopian flag is arguably the most influential flag in African history, serving as the inspiration for many other African nations, due to the colours green, yellow, and red being adopted by the Pan-Africanist movement. This is because of Ethiopia's position as the continent's oldest independent nation, and the inspiration from which other African nations have found in this flag and what it represents. The star motif in the middle, as Ethiopia's national emblem, represents unity between the people of Ethiopia, and its rays represent the nation's prospects.

19 - ANGOLA

Colour: 16   Design: 36

Identifiability: 32

Total: 84/100

Angola's flag is certainly distinctive amongst those of its neighbours, although that would appear to be both a blessing and a hinderance. The bold colour scheme and intriguing design certainly draw the attention, not to mention the machete that features in the flag's emblem. There is, however, an undeniably aggressive political nature to this flag, holding it back from the top spots.

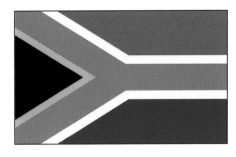

18 - SOUTH AFRICA

Colour: 10   Design: 34

Identifiability: 40

Total: 84/100

It may upset some people that South Africa's flag hasn't made it to the top 10, so allow me to clarify, this is a fantastic flag. It is one of the most well-known and loved flags of the entire world, and the vibrant colour scheme makes it stand out from the crowd. The use of six colours however contributes to the overall chaotic appearance of this flag.

17 - NORTH KOREA

Colour: 18   Design: 35

Identifiability: 32

Total: 85/100

A prime example of a country's placement in this list having no connection to its political standpoint, the flag of North Korea is one of the best, notably taking two commonly used shapes - a star and circle - and combining them to create a simple but unusual motif that gets the North Korean flag noticed. Perhaps a little on the boring side, but what this flag does, it does well.

16 - MARSHALL ISLANDS

Colour: 17   Design: 34

Identifiability: 35

Total: 86/100

One of several small Pacific island nations featuring in the top 20, the flag of the Marshall Islands is unlike any other national flag, without coming across as brash or excessive. The blue field illustrates the nations position as an island nation, and the orange and white stripes represent the equator, which isn't immediately obvious by the flag's orientation, but adds an interesting perspective to the flag.

15 - VANUATU

Colour: 14   Design: 35

Identifiability: 38

Total: 87/100

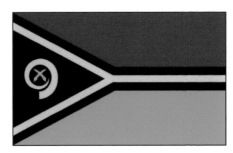

Vanuatu, one of the island nations of Oceania, is represented by this alluring flag. The emblem on the hoist side of the flag depicts a boars tusk, a significant symbol for the ni-Vanuatu people from the practice of islanders wearing the tusks as a status symbol, and also features crossed fern leaves, which are presented as a peace token. This flag is rich in meaning and depth, for a nation that many people in the world will be broadly unfamiliar with, so it is deserving of a high placement on this list. If the leaves in the emblem were less detailed, this flag would potentially make it to the top ten.

14 - ISRAEL

Colour: 14   Design: 33

Identifiability: 40

Total: 87/100

Israel's flag is one of the best examples of using simple imagery to memorably depict a country, with the Star of David in the center serving as the symbol for Judaism, and representing the unique culture and history of this nation. No fancy details, no unnecessary coat of arms, just an effective and well-thought-out design which it is almost impossible to confuse with any other national flag.

13 - GERMANY

Colour: 20   Design: 32

Identifiability: 35

Total: 87/100

The highest ranking plain tricolour flag by a considerable margin, Germany's flag is fully deserving of one of the top spots on this list, serving as a fantastic example of how the colours used in a country's flag can become very closely tied to the identity of that country. A lack of interesting design holds Germany back from the top 10, but nonetheless a great flag.

12 - ST. LUCIA

Colour: 16   Design: 37

Identifiability: 34

Total: 87/100

St. Lucia's flag isn't too showy or extravagant, with a simple design in the middle to get the flag noticed. The symbolism behind its triangular design, which may not be immediately obvious, represents the mountainous terrain of this Caribbean island - more specifically, it represents Gros Piton and Petit Piton, two peaks formed by hardened magma and providing popular tourist attractions for visitors to St. Lucia.

11 - BOSNIA AND HERZEGOVINA

Colour: 17   Design: 34

Identifiability: 36

Total: 87/100

Another great example of ignoring flag convention without it seeming uncomfortable or forced, the flag of Bosnia and Herzegovina is both proudly European, as depicted by the stars, and distinctively Bosnian, seen in the choices of colour and the triangle shape, similar to the shape of the country itself.

10 - UNITED KINGDOM

Colour: 18   Design: 30

Identifiability: 40

Total: 88/100

Few flags have become as iconic throughout world history as that of the UK, a bold and long-standing flag which is as satisfying and textured as it is meaningful. It combines the flags of the constituent countries at the time of its creation, hence Wales is not represented here, instead depicting the crosses of St. George, St. Andrew, and St. Patrick. To add any more detail to this flag would be excessive, and would be tampering with a flag that is practically universally recognised.

9 - BURUNDI

Colour: 15   Design: 34

Identifiability: 39

Total: 88/100

Certainly one of the lesser-known flags of Africa, the flag of Burundi is not to be overlooked. In this design, Burundi adapt the saltire pattern (the white 'x' shape) by placing a white circle in the middle, but beyond this, they add little additional detail to prevent the flag from looking cluttered or giving the viewer too much to concentrate on. The stars represent the three main ethnic groups of this Central African nation (the Hutu, Tutsi and Twa people), red represents the bloodshed in pursuit of freedom for Burundi, green is for hope for the future, and white is for peace.

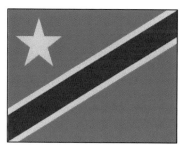

8 - D. R. CONGO

Colour: 18   Design: 35

Identifiability: 36

Total: 89/100

A staggering 160 places above the similarly named Republic of the Congo, the flag of the DRC is in a different league to that of its neighbour, achieving the seemingly elusive accolade of creating a flag which is both simple and eye-catching. Its design and vibrant colour scheme stand out (especially amongst many of its neighbours), although the meanings behind this imagery isn't particularly distinctive. The red represents the blood spilled on behalf of the country, the yellow represents wealth, and the blue represents peace.

7 - PAPUA NEW GUINEA

Colour: 16   Design: 33

Identifiability: 40

Total: 89/100

Another flag placed firmly in the 'cool' category, thanks mostly to the raggiana bird-of-paradise that features in the upper fly-side corner, Papua New Guinea's flag tells you most of what you need to know about the country without overstaying its welcome. The colours are bold, and the design is unusual and appealing.

6 - NAURU

Colour: 17   Design: 39

Identifiability: 34

Total: 90/100

This flag may appear to rank excessively high on this list, but hear me out. Many may not have even heard of this tiny island in the Pacific Ocean, with around 10,000 inhabitants and very few annual visitors, so it is fair to say that Nauru had little to work with when designing this flag. This is part of the charm of the Nauruan flag, which proudly boasts to the world two of the things this country is known for - its position just under the equator, and the phosphate reserves which gained Nauru international attention (represented in white).

5 - SEYCHELLES

Colour: 14   Design: 40

Identifiability: 36

Total: 90/100

Another example of a flag which has managed to stand out from the crowd without being overbearing, it's hard not to like the flag of the Seychelles. Colourful and optimistic, and unlike any other national flag, this archipelago in the Indian Ocean is represented by one of the worlds most well-loved flags.

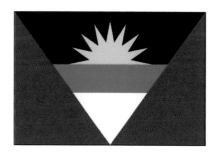

4 - ANTIGUA AND BARBUDA

Colour: 15   Design: 39

Identifiability: 36

Total: 90/100

The flag of Antigua and Barbuda does just about everything right. The small island nation in the Caribbean has a flag which is simultaneously distinctive and simplistic, as well as including considerately chosen symbolism. The flag was adopted after a nationwide competition in 1967 to redesign their flag, and it is easy to interpret was is being represented here.

3 - BARBADOS

Colour: 18   Design: 38

Identifiability: 35

Total: 91/100

Coming in at 3rd place is the flag of Barbados, with a simple but unique design that very obviously represents a Caribbean nation, with the blue depicting the Ocean, and yellow/gold depicting the sand. More striking however is the trident of Poseidon, the Greek god of the sea, unlike anything seen in other flags of the world. The trident was actually first featured in the colonial flag of Barbados under British rule, and their breakaway into independence is represented by the tridents handle being broken off.

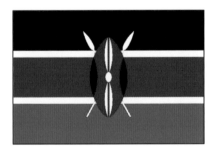

2 - KENYA

Colour: 15   Design: 39

Identifiability: 38

Total: 92/100

Ranking at 2nd place, and very deserving of this placement, is the flag of Kenya. The spears and Maasai shield that take pride of place on the Kenyan flag are perhaps the best example of iconography on a national flag, thoughtfully illustrating some of Kenyan culture in a way that is instantly noticeable without coming across as overbearing or overly complex. Some of the most meaningful symbolism and satisfying design that national flags have to offer.

1 - JAMAICA

Colour: 20 Design: 35

Identifiability: 40

Total: 95/100

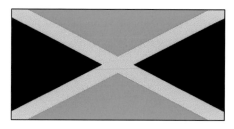

Easily taking the first-place spot on the list, and judged to be the best national flag in the world, is that of Jamaica. Interestingly, the Jamaican flag is the only national flag which does not make use of the colours red, white, or blue, with the colours it instead opts for having become practically synonymous with Jamaica itself.

The design, referred to as a 'saltire', is a relatively simplistic one, yet is rarely seen on the international stage, so it is immediately recognisable. As such, Jamaica's flag proves that a flags design does not need to be overly detailed or complex to stand out from the crowd, a feat achieved by seemingly few national flags.

In terms of symbolism, the yellow cross (officially 'gold') represents the sunlight and warm climate, as well as the nation's wealth, black represents the strong and creative people of Jamaica, and green represents hope and the vibrant natural landscape the country has to offer.

So, there you have it. Through the application of different principles in vexilology, the study of flags, Jamaica's has ended up on the top of this list, and I can't say that I am surprised. Flags are an incredibly important way of representing a country, and few do it quite so appealingly as Jamaica.

AND FINALLY...

Below are some statistics on these rankings which you might find interesting:

AFRICA CONTINENT SUMMARY

- Total of 54 countries
- Highest ranking country (2nd place, 92/100) - Kenya
- Lowest ranking country (193rd place, 27/100 - Benin
- Average score - 58.70

ASIA CONTINENT SUMMARY

- Total of 49 countries
- Highest ranking country (14th place, 87/100) - Israel
- Lowest ranking country (195th place, 24/100) - Indonesia
- Average score - 61.33

EUROPE CONTINENT SUMMARY

- Total of 45 countries
- Highest ranking country (10th place, 88/100) - UK
- Lowest ranking country (196th place, 23/100) - Monaco
- Average score - 60.82

NORTH AMERICA CONTINENT SUMMARY

- Total of 23 countries
- Highest ranking country (1st place, 95/100) - Jamaica
- Lowest ranking country (197th place, 22/100) - Haiti
- Average score - 65.96

(ONLY INCLUDING CARIBBEAN ISLAND NATIONS)

- Total of 12 countries
- Average score - 75.33

OCEANIA CONTINENT SUMMARY

- Total of 14 countries
- Highest ranking country (6th place, 90/100) - Nauru
- Lowest ranking country (167th place, 43/100) - Samoa
- Average score - 66.07

SOUTH AMERICA CONTINENT SUMMARY

- Total of 12 countries
- Highest ranking country (22nd place, 83/100) - Guyana
- Lowest ranking country (184th place, 35/100) - Bolivia
- Average score - 62.42

COLOURS SUMMARY

Top 3:
- Joint 1st - Jamaica, Germany, Estonia (20/20)

Bottom 3:
- 197th - Zambia (4/20)
- 196th - Sri Lanka (5/20)
- Joint 191st - South Sudan, Turkmenistan, Montenegro, Dominica, Haiti (6/20)

IDENTIFIABILITY SUMMARY

Top 3:
- Joint 1st - Jamaica, Brazil, United States, United Kingdom, Papua New Guinea, Israel, Spain, South Africa, Nepal, South Korea (40/40)

Bottom 3:
- Joint 195th - Madagascar, Indonesia, Monaco (5/40)

DESIGN SUMMARY

Top 3:

- 1st - Seychelles (40/40)
- Joint 2nd - Antigua and Barbuda, Kenya, Nauru (39/30)

Bottom 3:

- 197th - Monaco (4/40)
- Joint 194th - Indonesia, Poland, Saudi Arabia (5/40)

(For the sake of these statistics, Turkey and Cyprus were counted as part of Asia, and Russia was counted as part of Europe).

LOOKING FOR A SPECIFIC COUNTRY?

Below is an alphabetical list of all the countries in this list, and the page number where this country can be found.

Gabon - 23
(The) Gambia - 36
Georgia - 53
Germany - 93
Ghana - 55
Greece - 72
Grenada - 41
Guatemala - 22
Guinea - 8
Guinea-Bissau - 37
Guyana - 88
Haiti - 1
Holy See (see Vatican City)
Honduras - 31
Hungary - 19
Iceland - 87
India - 59
Indonesia - 2
Iran - 79
Iraq - 34
Ireland - 76
Israel - 92
Italy - 82
Ivory Coast - 11
Jamaica - 99
Japan - 69
Jordan - 52
Kazakhstan - 65
Kenya - 98
Kiribati - 67
Kosovo - 32
Kuwait - 53
Kyrgyzstan - 49
Laos - 21
Latvia - 7
Lebanon - 79

Lesotho - 69
Liberia - 80
Libya - 46
Liechtenstein - 6
Lithuania - 20
Luxembourg - 11
Macedonia (see North Macedonia)
Madagascar - 3
Malawi - 56
Malaysia - 71
Maldives - 4
Mali - 5
Malta - 13
Marshall Islands - 91
Mauritania - 9
Mauritius - 51
Mexico - 55
Micronesia - 39
Moldova - 13
Monaco - 1
Mongolia - 77
Montenegro - 30
Morocco - 10
Mozambique - 27
Myanmar - 29
Namibia - 64
Nauru - 96
Nepal - 80
(The) Netherlands - 44
New Zealand - 49
Nicaragua - 16
Niger - 4
Nigeria - 42
North Korea - 91
North Macedonia - 81
Norway - 88

Oman - 23

Pakistan - 60

Palau - 51

Palestine - 47

Panama - 61

Papua New Guinea - 96

Paraguay - 29

Peru - 9

(The) Philippines - 60

Poland - 2

Portugal - 66

Qatar - 58

Republic of the Congo - 15

Romania - 62

Russia - 45

Rwanda - 67

Saint Kitts and Nevis - 84

Saint Lucia - 93

Saint Vincent and the
Grenadines - 81

Samoa - 16

San Marino - 24

São Tomé and Principe - 40

Saudi Arabia - 21

Senegal - 20

Serbia - 42

Seychelles - 97

Sierra Leone - 47

Singapore - 35

Slovakia - 78

Slovenia - 58

Solomon Islands - 74

Somalia - 41

South Africa - 90

South Korea - 82

South Sudan - 12

Spain - 75

Sri Lanka - 48

Sudan - 43

Suriname - 70

Swaziland (see Eswatini)

Sweden - 75

Switzerland - 76

Syria - 56

Taiwan - 14

Tajikistan - 73

Tanzania - 78

Thailand - 68

Togo - 36

Tonga - 25

Trinidad and Tobago - 85

Tunisia - 33

Turkey - 32

Turkmenistan - 8

Tuvalu - 25

Uganda - 71

Ukraine - 12

United Arab Emirates - 38

United Kingdom - 94

United States - 87

Uruguay - 52

Uzbekistan - 54

Vanuatu - 92

Vatican City - 26

Venezuela - 77

Vietnam - 22

Yemen - 31

Zambia - 15

Zimbabwe - 37

ACKNOWLEDGEMENTS

There are a number of people I would like to thank for making this book possible.

Firstly, I wish to reiterate my thanks for those mentioned in the dedication at the beginning of this book, my good friends Solmaz, Michael and Tim, who gave me the idea for this book back in my first year of university. Thanks for listening to me talk endlessly about flags, for encouraging me to write this book, and for all the fun times we have had together.

The biggest 'thank you' of all goes to my parents, for the countless hours spend encouraging me to follow my passions and interests, for instilling in me strong values and beliefs, and most importantly teaching me to enjoy the life that I have. Thank you, Mum and Dad, and the rest of my family too.

Writing and producing a book has been a completely new experience for me, so a special thanks must go to those who have helped make this a reality. To Emma, who designed this wonderful cover art, to Jon, and his photography skills, and to Emma Jade, who talked me through the process of publishing a book.

Finally, thanks a lot to all of my friends who have been a part of this process. Far too many to name, but special thanks to the Hart family, my housemates, the 'CU' boys, the gals at 35, Lizzi, Jo, and anyone else who has been a part of the process. You da best.

ABOUT THE AUTHOR

Max Hall, hailing from Kent, is a Christian, honorary Brightonian, and long-time geography fanatic. From a young age, he has had a fond interest in countries, capital cities, and yes indeed flags. After an evening on the student radio station at university with some good friends, and an impromptu flag guessing game, this book was suggested. Three years (and one degree) later, Max eventually got around to compiling and publishing this list, the product of which you are holding in your hands. So… thank you for being a part of this.

(Image by Jonathan Somarib, @photosomarib)

Printed in Great Britain
by Amazon

43659533R00067